A HOUSE NAMED
SIMPLICITY

A HOUSE NAMED
SIMPLICITY

Stories of Finding Home

Susan Eaton Mendenhall

Shanti Arts Publishing
Brunswick, Maine

A House Named Simplicity
Stories of Finding Home

Copyright © 2021 Susan Eaton Mendenhall
All Rights Reserved
No part of this book may be used or reproduced in any manner whatsoever without the written permission of the publisher except for the use of brief quotations in a book review.

Published by Shanti Arts Publishing
Interior and cover design by Shanti Arts Designs

Shanti Arts LLC
193 Hillside Road
Brunswick, Maine 04011
shantiarts.com

Paintings by Susan Eaton Mendenhall; photographs by Don and Susan Eaton Mendenhall; used with their permission.

This is a work of non-fiction. The events and conversations recounted in this book come from the author's best recollections and are presented in a way that evokes the feeling and meaning of the experience at that time.

ISBN: 978-1-951651-68-8 (softcover)
ISBN: 978-1-951651-69-5 (ebook)

Library of Congress Control Number: 2020952842

To Don,

*each day with you is a gift
and an adventure.*

Contents

Acknowledgments — 11
Introduction — 15

1 Meeting Number Five — 19
2 Simplifying! — 27
3 Naming Her — 33
4 Voices — 39
5 Two Boats — 45
6 Morning Pages — 51
7 From Work to Caring — 57
8 Soaking in the Tub — 61
9 Chair Tales — 65
10 Kitchen Wisdom — 71

11 Rocks — 75
12 The Conversation — 79
13 Simplicity's Hospitality — 87
14 Sharing Space, Sharing Lives — 93
15 Simplicity's Versatility — 99
16 Dear Artist — 103
17 Studio Space — 107
18 Art on the Walls — 113
19 Dream for Artist Space — 117
20 A New Door — 121

21	Storage–Where Stuff Lies in Darkness and Indecision	125
22	One Thing Leads to Another	129
23	Old House Syndrome	133
24	More Than a Table	137
25	Block Party	141
26	The Porches	145
27	Our 10 x 10 Home	149
28	A Smile Goes a Long Way	155
29	Becoming a Grandparent House	159
30	Going Up Going Down	165
31	Twice a Day	169
32	Check List	173
33	Time to Leave?	177
34	Moving Furniture	181
35	Pottery	185
36	The Tall Blonde	189
37	A House is Found	193
38	Simplifying Christmas	199
39	More Than a Junk Drawer	203
40	Jinxed	209
41	Simplicity is For Sale	215
42	Love Letter to Simplicity	219
43	SOLD!	223
44	Downsizing?	227
45	Waiting Anxiously	231
46	Living In-Between	235
47	From Katharine to Phoebe	239

48	One Happy House Left	243
49	Saying Good-Bye	247
50	Each House Holds a Story	251

Epilogue	257
Discussion Questions for Book Groups or Personal Reflection	261
Conversation Starters	263
Resources	265
About the Author	269

Acknowledgments

◆ ◆ ◆

WHEN I READ MAY SARTON'S *PLANT DREAMING Deep*, I found a woman who spoke of her house as I spoke of Simplicity. Each chapter of her book offered gems to my understanding of house and home and the unique relationship between house and owner. Being a writer, she wondered whether an old farmhouse was a place where poetry would come to her. I wondered if Simplicity was a place where I could find my purpose. For both of us, as we came to know our homes, we came to know ourselves.

For years, I said, "I must write this story." For years, I didn't. When I finally tired of my own words and empty promises, I became serious. Knowing I needed all the nudging possible to make this book happen, I joined three writing groups, took classes, found writing partners, and hired a writing coach, Julie Tallard Johnson.

I gave myself three years to write Simplicity's story. My commitment began as a weekly blog. Writing about Simplicity was a joy, and posting every Thursday demanded accountability. To get away from the distractions and procrastinations that occurred at home, I frequently stayed at my daughter's apartment, found coffee shops, quiet libraries, and B & B's where I could write. My husband, Don, listened and helped me remember these stories we lived together.

So many people contributed to the making of this book. For each one of them I am grateful.

When I visualized the format for *A House Named Simplicity: Stories of Finding Home*, I knew I wanted each story to begin with a quotation. As a collector of quotations, I have included some of my favorites. Again, gratitude to the many authors who penned these meaningful and succinct phrases.

If I were reading this book, I would want to "see" the stories. A glimpse of Simplicity through a black and white sketch seemed perfect. The sketches were created from photographs taken by Don and me as well as paintings I made of Simplicity while we lived in her. May both the quotations and sketches add to your enjoyment in reading these stories.

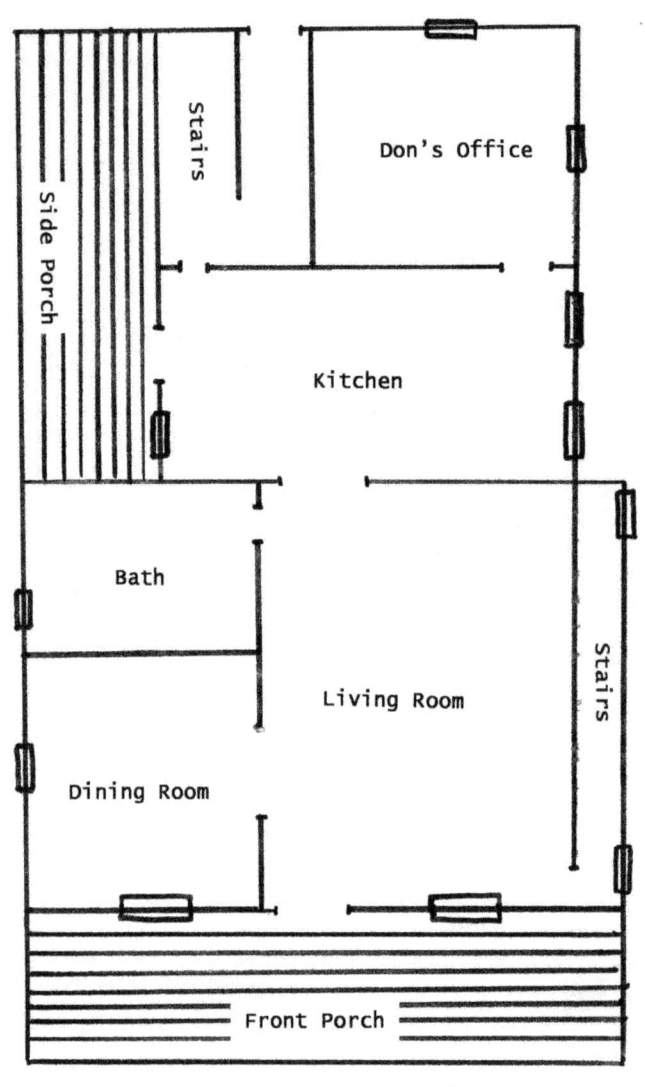

Sketch of First Floor

Introduction

A House Named Simplicity is a collection of stories about a house that supported our quest to find home, both in a place and within ourselves. Don and I asked much of this house we called Simplicity. At every turn she granted us an opportunity to enrich our lives and the lives of others. She offered a place to dream and a place to seek refuge. Simplicity was an old house that found a new life, just as we did.

From my childhood bedroom to our current home, changing and rearranging rooms has been a passion. Rooms get re-named, furniture and objects moved, added, eliminated. I love finding the intention of space. Where is the best place to read a book? The most supportive place to write? How to organize a room to facilitate group conversation or the most intimate sharing between two people? How to be efficient in use and upkeep? How will lighting impact the atmosphere? Where and how to hang artwork? These are the reoccurring questions that shape the supportive spaces in my life.

When we bought Simplicity, we discovered she had much to share in the questions we asked of her. As a writer I documented how she affected me, our marriage, family and friends, our work lives. As a painter I painted her. Each time I approached the canvas or paper, I asked her what she had to tell me, what to pay attention to, to notice, how to paint her. Some days she asked me to paint her strong American Four-Square structure or see her unique qualities or feel the many lives she has held over the years. On other days she was silent, waiting for me to find my story in all she offered.

Because of her wisdom and unique personality, she became a teacher, mentor and friend. In time I discovered that her wisdom was not only for me, but others who also seek a sense of place, an intention of home, an intimacy with the spaces that surround them. As has been my life pattern, I find meaning and solace in the places I live. My homes help define me. As you enter Simplicity's rooms and stories, may you discover more about yourself and the place you call home.

Susan Eaton Mendenhall

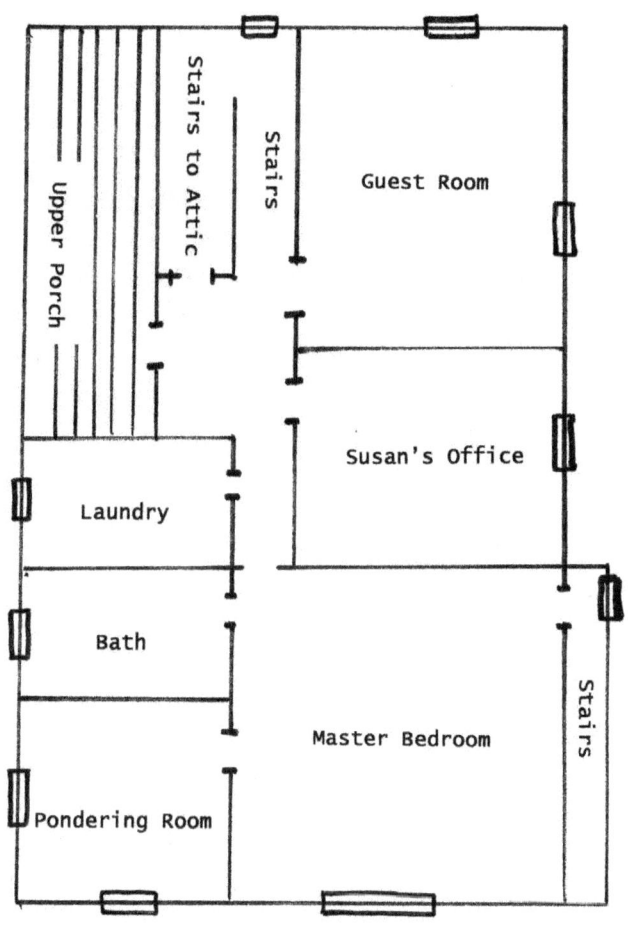

Sketch of Second Floor

Places speak to us. What they say affects us and influences our behaviour. Their messages stem from the underlying attitudes with which places are planned, made, used, and maintained. Few of us consciously acknowledge these messages, but subliminally we all experience them, are all affected by them.

♦ Christopher Day, *Spirit and Place*

1

Meeting Number Five

◆ ◆ ◆

OUR EYES SCANNED THE BLOCK FROM THE realtor's slow-moving car. Was our home in this mix of two stories, ranches, older and newer houses seen through the window? A year's worth of looking had not produced a single place we wanted to call home. We had looked at new construction and houses built in every decade. Houses located in rural and urban settings, in a variety of neighborhoods, a host of towns. Nothing yet felt like home, our home.

Five houses were seen on that day in March when the Midwest skies were flat gray and the cold felt heavy. Specifically, five houses built before 1950 in hopes of seeing older homes with character. There was exhaustion with the lingering conclusion of winter, not only in the air, but in our bones. Finding a home had been much more complicated than expected.

I promise to create a home with you, space for us to dream, explore, grow, and love. A safe place for our hearts' passions. These were words Don and I promised each other on our honeymoon in Assisi, Italy. As we walked down each of the steep stone steps found in the middle of town, we took turns speaking our promises and listening to the other. Thirty-six steps, thirty-six intentions for our life together. This was a new marriage, a new start later in life. Both of us had lived decades in previous marriages, raised children, divorced, and then found a soulmate in the other. Having lived apart for two years due to jobs in different states and one year together in a small apartment, this three-year marriage needed a place to call home.

Our current apartment life was adventurous, even playful. Overjoyed at finally being together, the apartment had been our tutorial in living together. Here we learned more about each other's daily habits, preferences, and energies. Here we dreamed and planned our life forward. Everything about the next chapter of life felt exciting and hopeful, but I was soon to discover, not easy.

I was surprised to find myself restless. The restlessness revolved around work, or in my case, lack of work. Don was employed and had a network of friends and business connections. I had left a job that energized me, plus a support system of friends and family. I was confident the next perfect job would show up. With an updated resume, I stretched into a variety of different vocational avenues, was interviewed but not hired. Both relief and disappointment accompanied this reality. No job fit. For a time, I found random bits of work doing leadership workshops. Fascinated by words such as integrity, communication, and clarity, as well as quotations about leadership, I wondered what these words and phrases would look like using paints and brushstrokes. This was the start of my painting style known as JazzArt, a creative outlet, but not financially sustainable. Struggling to find a meaningful vocation, I knew deep within that I would be okay. What I did not know or anticipate was how long and difficult this struggle would be. I hoped that finding a place to call home would settle me, end the restlessness, both external and internal.

The first house seen on this cold winter's day was a rambling Victorian. Begging for us to notice its charming potential, what we saw was a sloping porch and countless repairs. House number one had us calculating the dollars to make it livable to our needs and standards. We easily said no and moved onto house number two, a dark red brick bungalow built in the 1930s. The pleasing exterior of house number two was quickly forgotten when we opened the door and stepped inside. What were considered upgrades had been slapped together in haphazard, make-shift ways. Quality by any definition was missing. Woods didn't match. Doors were of varying styles. Walls looked dismal with worn wallpaper and chipped paint. One of the bedrooms was painted black. While the house was empty of its former owners, their lives lingered in their lack of care for the house. Such a relief to close the door on this one. Houses three and four proved to be dull and uneventful, without any story to tell. As we walked through, there was no attraction. Charisma and charm were absent. Thus far we had seen older homes needing work and deep pockets of money to renovate. Our hearts were weary. Would we ever find a place to call home?

The realtor's car stopped in front of house number five, a two-story American Foursquare built in 1905, a style of architecture that is boxy, simple and pragmatic. The house sat in the middle of a block, stark naked with no landscaping, just dirt and weeds. We learned from our realtor it had been moved to this location when the village center was redeveloped. Spared from the wrecking ball, two men saw her potential and gave her a new life. After being moved and renovated, it was sold. The owners never moved in. Once again for sale, the house sat empty for a year. Why, we wondered?

For a year we had been searching for a house, a home.

Was this the one? As a transplant to this neighborhood, number five did not look out of place, rather it belonged. Older homes were on either side and mature trees hugged the lot. Joining the other mix of houses on the block, this one fit perfectly into place, looked confident, even stately, with an elegance that brought smiles to our faces. The simplicity and wholesomeness of this house triggered our interest. New wheat colored siding, large white framed windows, front and side porches reaching out from her two-story frame. A recently poured cement driveway led to a detached garage and a welcoming sidewalk curved to her front door. Everything invited us in.

We stepped onto the open side porch. Floorboards freshly painted dark green, new white spindles and railings, gave this outdoor room a pleasing facelift. I envisioned a porch swing at one end. Simple and plain, nothing modern. Was it wrong to imagine, I wondered? Of course not. That's what this house hunting was all about. Could we see ourselves living in this place? This very particular place?

The door off the porch led us into a large kitchen that stretched across the full width of the house. Sunlight from the tall long windows spilled joy into the room and onto a beautifully aged maple floor. With its pristine white cabinets and dark green counter tops, the kitchen almost smelled like a pine forest in winter. Ten-foot ceilings gave a spaciousness to the room, inviting me to take a deep breath. I looked more closely. Noting the empty spaces for the appliances, I envisioned them white and in place. The refrigerator was planned to be across the room from the kitchen sink. I wondered if this would be an issue. A center island bridged the gap between the refrigerator and sink, easing my earlier concern. I noticed that the island was not designed to store stools underneath. We would need a small table and chairs. Where would they go? Quickly, I spotted two possible places.

"This is it! This is home!" Don's energetic voice penetrated my silent problem solving. My head turned to look at him. His smiling face exuded confidence and clarity. While I had to agree the first impression was positive, even exciting, I was not ready to claim this old house as home. Only the kitchen had been seen. Disappointment could be lurking in the next room, on the second floor. What might we find that would be a deal breaker? Thus far, our house search had been one disappointment after another. What made Don say that, I wondered? How could he be sure so soon? And if he felt it, why didn't I?

"Really?" I managed to respond. "What makes you say that?"

"It feels like home," was all he could identify at the time. A year later he discovered the reason why. While looking at old photos he came across one of his beloved grandparents' home, a house with nearly the same floor plan, only flipped.

I suggested we move into the next room, keep exploring each empty space. The beautifully restored wooden floors from the kitchen continued throughout the house and led us on a respectful journey room after room. We took our time, looking with experienced eyes and hopeful hearts. Windows and doorways had wide hardwood outlines, simple, but not plain. Without draperies, carpeting, or furniture, no filter was needed to see the basic frame of this house. There was no sofa pattern, wall art or ghastly colored walls to ignore or influence our seeing. What a gift to see a home void of a previous occupant, freshly prepared for the next. There was no other life to try not to see, only our life to imagine. For the first time in our year long search, optimism was palatable. I, too, could feel the sense of home beginning to enter my soul.

The bare spaces spoke to us. *What will you do with me?* each room asked. *Have you noticed my strong structure and good bones? I know I am old, a bit beaten up in places, but do you see my inner beauty, my potential? Are you here for a long while or will you fix me up then quickly sell? What are your intentions for me?* The spaces spoke with honesty. Simple and unpretentious, this house had an experienced past it was not hiding from us. It had lived other lives. Prior to being moved to this location and remodeled, the once family home had been sectioned off into a barber shop / hair salon, a tailor's workspace, and a rental apartment. Restored to a single-family dwelling, it was awaiting a new beginning, just as we were.

Don and I spend countless hours talking about how we wish to live, work, and play. This kind of philosophical and practical conversation is one we share over a meal, a morning cup of coffee, and on road trips with miles of highway before us. We dream. We diagram. We decide. Buying a house without a plan of how we would live there was unthinkable to us. This house was to hold the space for our artistic endeavors. Don's photography, my new pursuit of painting, we were writers. Our house needed to welcome family and friends for overnight stays, give space for offices, and have a floor plan that supported and inspired how we lived and worked. Both of us were re-inventing ourselves, not only in our marriage but in our blended families, work pursuits, and artistic nudges. We were looking for both the practical and the spiritual in a home. The house needed to have character, a sense of beauty, a pleasing simplicity. It needed to bring us to life in innovative ways, keep us interested and intrigued. It needed to help us find a sense of home within ourselves. Our lives were transitioning, re-arranging differently than before, and we were fully aware that an important ingredient was the place where we lived. Finding a place that knew about change, letting go, and re-inventing itself, was perfect.

My mind was spinning with practical questions. Would our furniture, our sense of design fit here? Which room would be the guest room? How would we enter the house, by the back door or the side porch? My heart was full of feelings. Comfort, excitement, anticipation, eagerness, a peace that we had finally found a place to call home. There was nothing the house was trying to hide from us and I found myself trusting its honesty, its simple nature. This house felt right, matched our yearning to live simply while stretching us into new lives.

"This feels like us, doesn't it, Don?" My voice was finally able to speak the words I was experiencing.

"It does. It feels like home."

While listening to her spaces, we found ourselves committing our souls to a simple house. Without hesitation we promised her our love, to honor her structural integrity, to breathe new life into her. She promised to accommodate our hopes and dreams, with a willingness to learn new ways of supporting our lifestyles and hospitality. Suddenly it was difficult to think of our lives without the wisdom of this house. To us, home was a sacred partnership between house and owner. On that cold day in March, Don and I found a house. Now to create a home.

Have nothing in your houses that you do not know to be useful or believe to be beautiful.

◆ William Morris, *Hopes and Fears for Art:
Five Lectures Delivered in Birmingham,
London, and Nottingham, 1878–1881*

2

Simplifying!

♦ ♦ ♦

A YEAR BEFORE WE BOUGHT HOUSE NUMBER FIVE, our two households came together. The combined assortment of boxed memories, books, furniture, collections, and decor was simplified to fit in a two-bedroom apartment. Knowing Don's job at the time was a two-year position, we wanted to be able to relocate easily and readily, not encumbered with a house to sell or too much stuff to move. What if a professional move took us to another city, across the country, to another country? Renting an apartment was the solution.

Our loft apartment was numbered 2B, a number that coincidentally spoke to our situation. What was "to be" for us? In the first two years of marriage, our work kept us living in two different houses, in two different states. Finally, we were together. Both in our fifties and one marriage each behind us, we had well developed patterns of how we lived. Putting ourselves in this small space was the first experiment.

Other than the five-foot-square room provided in the garage, a strategic decision was made not to rent an additional storage unit. Too much storage space felt like a deliberate act of procrastination and an easy place to put the undecideds. At the same time, it was crucial that our apartment not feel stuffed or cluttered. We agreed there would be no stacks of boxes piled in the corner or furniture squeezed in because we could make it fit. Having only what we needed and nothing more was our desire, however, where to begin felt daunting. What would go? What would stay? Don saves. I toss. How would we ever come to a mutual agreement? I began to see a very lengthy process of every item being held up, scrutinized, and evaluated. Overwhelm sat with us. A plan was desperately needed.

We decided to ask ourselves three questions as a place to begin: What items have a needed function? What items add beauty into our lives? What items remind us of our essence?

Function. Beauty. Essence. These words, these questions required both heart and mind to be activated. Unsure how this process would unfold with items we cherished and loved, we asked ourselves to be extra tender with the other and very aware of our own feelings. We reminded each other that we could make this work.

Function involved whether an item or piece of furniture was needed, required for basic living. Often this was case specific and easy. Why do we need four potato peelers? Other times the decision was muddy and unclear. Such was the case of our eclectic assortment of end tables. Don's had a modern boxy style with use of glass and metal. Those from my house were in rich woods, more classic and unique. Each one was functional, but we didn't need them all. Which ones felt like they matched the home we were creating? Those kinds of questions found us pressing the pause button and talking it out. Always, the decision was stronger and clearer. We bid farewell to the boxy moderns.

Beauty enhanced our everyday, elevated our

thoughts and moods. Artwork was placed in the beauty category—photographs, sculpture, and paintings. Sometimes the shape and style of a lamp bumped it more securely into our functional choice because it also had beauty. Don's hammered pewter lamp was stunning. The round base with rhythmic and repeated markings was pleasing and calming. It stayed. My bronze angular Asian influenced lamp also stayed. Tall like a stretched ginger jar, the angular edges gave it distinction. We said good-bye to the see-through glass and boring desk lamps. Well used, functional for those early days when they were the only lamps we had, it was easy to let them go. Dishes, glassware, trays, and pottery that were considered attractive ranked higher than those that were simply functional. The beautiful stayed.

Essence encouraged our creative and artistic souls. For Don, that meant many of his photography books, vintage and current cameras, a carving of his patron saint, St Francis, made by his mentor, Aunt Ellen. For me, that included items for the home that made homemaking an art form. The wooden dining room table and chairs with their dark cranberry red stained legs represented the importance of sharing stories and lingering over a meal. An ivy plant honoring a friendship was making the move as was a set of cream-colored Wedgewood dishes once belonging to my beloved Aunt Dorothy. She exemplified hospitality. Every meal served on these elegantly modest dishes made the experience rich and special. Sprigs of parsley adorned the plate, coffee served in demitasse cups, and her sterling silverware turned a simple meal into a luxurious one. For both of us, books that were touchstones throughout our lives joined this category. Dag Hammarskjold, Margaret Wheatley, Parker

Palmer, Krishnamurti, Eleanor Roosevelt, and select others were packed lovingly into a box for the move to 2B.

With Don and I fully invested in this simplifying practice, a fourth question, with its close partner, showed up to help. Am I done with this? Has it served its purpose? Books and resources used in our earlier vocations, notes of appreciation, swimming trophies and medals, documents that kept our lives safe and secure. Once again, the words "to be or not to be" were our guide.

Don's giraffe collection fell into this category. Had it served its purpose?

Collections are a different lot, often uncontrollable, a creative outlet that engages lives like a treasure hunt without a map. Mind you, it was never Don's intention to begin this collection. It just happened, starting with a visit to Africa when he brought back two large papier-mâché giraffes. Then they began arriving. For birthdays. For special recognitions. On cards. On wall hangings. On mugs. Made of glass, of metal, of wood. That's the nature of a collection, it grows. Family, friends and colleagues catch the collecting spirit and add their favorites. The exact number? Over one hundred. Each giraffe beautiful and unique. Where would they find a home in our small two-bedroom apartment? He thoughtfully reduced the field to five.

We recognized that this simplifying process was not only lightening our load but redefining our lives. We let go of the items we had outgrown, that no longer fit who we were. The result was keeping the pieces we most loved, that gave us life and energy in moving forward. We found ourselves revitalized in our separate lives, our marriage, and our shared space. It felt as if the best of each of us showed up in the items that stayed. They were offerings, gifts, dowries for our life together.

Once our decisions were made, we held a colossal garage sale. Don specifically noted his giraffe collection in the publicity. Sure enough, the very first person to show up that morning was one who himself had a giraffe collection. He bought them all. It seemed a most suitable ending.

The almost absolute lack of elaborate detail is one of the chief charms of this residence. Its elegance is its simplicity.

> ♦ a description of the American Foursquare found in the April 1899 *Ladies Home Journal*

3

Naming Her

◆ ◆ ◆

I ADMIT KNOWING NOTHING ABOUT AMERICAN Foursquare architecture before buying one. But I was curious and did some research. After the detailed and elaborate architecture of the Victorian and Queen Anne homes, Americans were ready for practicality. With a new century just around the corner, the American Foursquare supported a changing lifestyle that was less sophisticated and more sensible, moving from detailed ornamentation to clean minimalism in a dwelling that was humble, understated, and unpretentious. The style became the affordable middle-class home, even available as a pre-ordered kit through Sears Roebuck and Company.

With a dossier of identifiable characteristics, the American Foursquare style is easy to recognize. Common features are a two-and-a half-story structure, squared rooms, single dormer in the roof line, an open porch across the entire width of the house, large front windows, and interior doors with five inset panels. A practical, economical, comfortable, and efficient house. These were the values Don and I try to live in our everyday ordinary way.

"How do you feel about naming this house?" I asked Don.

Having named my last house, I was rather keen on the idea, but unsure of Don's thoughts on the matter. Giving a house a name gave it a personality, established a closer relationship between owner and house. I relished that kind of partnership with a home and hoped Don did too.

"I like that idea. What fun to think of just the right name," he shared and already was going into that creative mood I love about him. Our English heritage reminded us that before numbers and official addresses were established, houses were named. The names were indicative of some aspect of their geography, architectural structure or family lineage.

There was an aspect of this house that we especially appreciated—simplicity. This was also a value we continually sought to integrate into our lives by less consumerism and an interest in minimalism. Simplicity spoke to us of being present and intentional. The clean lines of this house prompted us to see and respect the gift of enough, not only in our home but in our emerging artwork and busy lives. We were determined to keep the spaciousness of each room rather than to fill them with too much. In the words of Thomas Moore: "Simplicity doesn't mean meagerness, but rather a certain kind of richness, the fullness that appears when we stop stuffing the world with things." That sentiment resonated. The name—Simplicity—suited the structure of this house and us. Simplicity became a "she" and a personality that would mid-wife our new life together.

If you give a house a name, doesn't she deserve a party? Resembling a baby's christening, we called it a house blessing. According to the Oxford English Dictionary, "to bless" means "to confer well-being upon," "to make happy," "to prosper." We invited those who had remodeled and sold us the house, the neighbors on either side who had sacrificed land for Simplicity's arrival, the realtor who worked with us to find the perfect home, and friends who were witnesses to the ups and downs of our yearlong house hunt.

Prior to everyone's arrival we readied Simplicity for her honored guests. Every corner was thoughtfully cleaned. Each interior room and exterior space were smudged with sage to refresh her and release any old energy that may have stagnated from her former lives. Candles were placed in the center of every room. Wisconsin cheeses, wine, fresh apple cider, grapes, walnuts, homemade chocolate chip cookies, and fresh bread just out of the oven welcomed one and all. Simplicity's spaces were alive with light, luscious smells, and love.

The guests who gathered that evening were new to each other, brought together because they held part of the story of this house or the story of our search. Everyone admitted that this was their first house blessing and were curious. I had prepared a list of quotations about home and sacred space to share with our guests. Architect Anthony Lawler, in his book *A Home for the Soul*, described home in this way: "Home offers a practical setting for fostering soul in concrete ways. It serves the requirements of shelter and food while simultaneously addressing our deeper needs for love, wisdom, and establishing a place in the world." From Victoria Moran in her book *Shelter for the Spirit*: "Home is where you go to refuel—physically, emotionally, and spiritually." From Winifred Gallagher's *House Thinking*: "Designers wonder 'How does it (a place) look?' The rest of us ask, 'How does it make me feel? Does it meet my needs?'" Our guests engaged in thoughtful conversation and offered words that meant home to them: a place to be yourself and relax; a place to feel safe, cozy, and peaceful; a sanctuary, and a place where stories are lived and hospitality is offered to visitors.

We explained we were naming her Simplicity in hopes that her minimal design would support us to live more simply, more intentionally. Guests were invited to move throughout the house, pause in each of the rooms to offer a thought, a prayer, a blessing for how that specific space might enhance our lives with the qualities of home. In both serious and playful ways, our guests blessed our home with love. The evening concluded over tasty refreshments and hearing each other's stories of finding home. We gathered that night to bless a house named Simplicity and call her home.

The house had already begun to feel inhabited by all kinds of presences besides my own.

♦ May Sarton, *Plant Dreaming Deep*

4

Voices

◆ ◆ ◆

WHEN YOU PURCHASE A HOUSE, YOU ALSO inherit unique sounds in and around that place. With Simplicity, we inherited the jet noise as planes began their descent into the Madison airport, train horns and sirens of emergency vehicles moving through the village center. These demanding noises were balanced by the energetic sounds of children at play in the nearby schoolyard, the cardinals calling back and forth to their partners, the red squirrels clucking as they sat on tree branches outside our windows. Inside, the sump pump belched, starting with a wheeze and ending with a thud. Old stairs creaked and moaned, each with its own audible response to a footstep. Some wall switches clicked, while others popped. As the bathroom door closed, the squeak in the hinge changed into a rub on the floor. Floorboards throughout the house spoke in high and low tones. The sounds heightened awareness of our surroundings, informed us about our home, our neighborhood, and village. Soon all sounds became familiar and expected. Except for one.

We heard voices. People talking inside the house. At first, we wondered if we had left on the television or radio; or were we overhearing the neighbors in the yard.

We searched the house from top to bottom, every nook and cranny. Nothing was on; no neighbors were in the yard. Maybe we had imagined it? We heard it again.

We narrowed the location of the voices to a room on the first floor. The moment we stepped into the room, they stopped. Who were these voices? Where did they come from? Did they belong to the house, live here? Were they going to stay? Question after question kept coming, arriving without an answer.

As we sat with these unknowns, we realized we were not frightened by these voices, but intrigued and curious. Never having had such an experience, we were unsure whether to approach this as a problem or an opportunity. With an unrealized dream of being great detectives, likely fed by the number of British murder mysteries we watch, Don and I thought of this as a mystery to be solved. Here we had a case that required analytical thinking as well as an adventuresome spirit. With our imaginary little black notebooks, magnifying glasses, and inquiring minds, our search for the answer began.

First, there was no crisis or alarm in the voices. They did not sound like cruel or malicious voices. Could we detect a specific word or phrase? Decipher a clue to help us understand why they were here? Not a single distinguishable word could be heard. More like background noise, except the background of what, of where? We guessed them to be women's voices as they had a higher pitch than a man's voice. Curious that we only heard the voices during the day, never at night, we continued to listen and note our findings. We also began to wonder what we were going to do about it. We had heard of house exorcisms, but these voices were not mean-spirited. Were they lost? Were they asking something of us, and if so, what?

After a month or two, there was a development in the case. Don and I began to wonder if Simplicity's history held a clue. I had read Stewart Brand's *How Buildings Learn: What Happens After They're Built*. The title and its contents fascinated me. The idea that buildings learn is an interesting concept and made sense. Buildings learn all the time. Take Simplicity, for example. Built around the turn of the century as a family home, it served in that capacity for years. Then, as the neighborhood changed, the use of the house did as well. It learned to be a hair salon and tailor shop on the lower level with a rental apartment on the upper floor. When major changes happened in the development of our village, it was scheduled to be demolished. Two men saw her potential and saved Simplicity by moving her to a new neighborhood. Once again it learned to be a single-family dwelling.

With one of her prior lives as a hair salon, were these the voices of those who came to have their hair done? Were these the conversations they had with each other as they sat in the stylist's chair or in the waiting room? Were they grieving the loss of a place that was safe and familiar? We were uncertain of any of this. Mostly curious.

The voices continued, and Don and I remained clueless as to what to do. One morning, hearing them, I stepped into the room we thought was their source. As was their pattern, they became silent. Suddenly, I began speaking to them, something that had not occurred to me before that very moment.

I want you to know we hear you. This move, these changes, must be difficult for you. Nothing is like it once was. Please know that Don and I love this house too. She is special and we will care for her. Stay as long as you must. We will not harm or force you to go.

As I spoke, I took stock of my words. What I had shared was true. The words had come from the heart. This was a place we desired to make into a home. This was a place with previous lives. I felt empathy for all the changes this house had endured, and I was surprised by my sense of compassion. Taking a deep breath, I left the room.

We never heard the voices again.

Fourteen years later, we were hosting our annual block party. The village police had been invited to talk about neighborhood watch and community involvement. One of the officers recognized our house as the one moved from the village center.

"I was part of the police escort," he shared matter-of-factly. Then both his facial expression and words hesitated, as if wondering whether he should continue. "I heard the original buyers never moved in, backed out of the deal," he offered after a pause.

His voice quieted. He took a deep breath as he raised his eyebrows. "I was told the house had voices."

You don't have to be in the same boat to journey together.

♦ The Mendenhall Mantra

5

Two Boats

◆ ◆ ◆

Photographs of two boats hung side by side in Simplicity's living room. One photograph was taken on a lake in Michigan by Don. The other I took on a study trip to China. Together, the photographs captured two simple rowboats side by side. The symbolism of two boats is integral to our story.

After Don and I decided to marry, the decision presented to many women at marriage rested heavily on my heart. Would I take Don's name, keep my own, or create a new name? I found my identity at stake. Because I was professionally known and published by the name from my previous marriage, there was a justifiable reason to keep it as it was. In the same breath, this name also reflected a previous relationship, a previous life that was no longer mine. My heart experienced a sense of loss while thinking about this.

To change one's name is cumbersome, requiring volumes of paperwork, re-introducing yourself, and paying attention to the many ways your new name impacts both the formal and informal parts of a life. One must remember who knows you by what name or adding "formerly" when offering your old name. Exhausting work, all the while adjusting to the present-day you with a different name.

As I sat with this decision, it became clear that to let go of my former married name was a way of moving forward.

With one name eliminated, the choices before me were taking Don's last name of Mendenhall, truly a beautiful name in and of itself, or creating my own unique name. I was also very aware that my independent self was resistant to go with the accepted pattern of a woman taking her husband's name. I could return to my maiden name, and looking through my genealogy, I found several other options to consider. Yet I felt ready for something new. Don was most sympathetic to my distress over this, agreeing that men have no clue to the identity struggle and hassle in updating records and accounts that a name change presents for women. Eager to be helpful and supportive, he suggested that I might also wish to give thought to becoming a one-name person, like Cher or Prince or Pink.

"You could pull this off," he smiled with twinkling eyes, giving me confidence to give this more serious thought. If I did become a one name person, what one name would sum me up? With a love of water and an easy-going nature, I settled on the name River.

My enthusiasm to share this epiphany happened over a lunch that included my daughter and a few of her ninth-grade girlfriends. To get them on board, I laid out my dilemma. I must admit that I was also attempting to offer an alternative or at least an awareness of this quandary for women, one that they themselves would likely face someday. At just the right moment, with a deep pause to give even further dramatic effect, I spoke my one-word name. River. My young tablemates smiled courteously. They nodded in agreement that surely River was a possible name given all that I had explained. My daughter, a "speak it like it is" kind of gal, allowed for the polite silence and then blurted, "Mom, if we were to call you River, it would sound like calling the family dog."

It stung at first, but I had to admit there was truth in her words. The reaction also accompanied my other questions about the name River. Would I tire or outgrow this name? Was it a name worthy of all the legal hoop jumping to make it happen? It became clear that River was not going to be my new name, but Mendenhall was still not convincing. My lawyer had suggested complications if I went the route of an entirely different name with no association to previous names of mine. I remained uncertain for several more weeks, delaying our marriage license because I had not yet decided what I was to be called in this relationship. I was a woman without a name. Remembering the difficulty in choosing the names of my children, this was similar and yet seemingly more complex.

On a summer afternoon, Don and I settled by the shores of Lake Wingra to write our marriage vows. Looking out onto the water, I saw a man in a yellow kayak followed by a woman in her own yellow kayak. It was obvious they were together, going toward the same destination, but had given each other space and autonomy by being in separate boats. As if touched by a magic wand, I knew what to do. The answer was clear, and I felt confident. I would legally become Susan Eaton Mendenhall, which included my maiden name, and I would craft another name, one that was personal and unique to me.

As I shared this awareness with Don, we both started playing with words and names. The moment he said "JAZZ," I knew that was the one. Jazz was filled with energy, excitement, creativity, movement, and independence. A name that invites me to color outside the lines, challenges my first born responsible nature of doing what is proper and expected. Jazz was alive and in the moment. This was exactly the way I felt in my relationship with Don, in this season of life. Jazz matched the style of my artwork and quickly became my artist name. Jazz awakened me to myself.

The photographs of two boats on Simplicity's wall spoke to this defining moment in our story. They recalled the day we sat on the shores of Lake Wingra, seeing two identical kayaks and experiencing it as a celebration of both our independence and mutual journey. The two boats remind us to respect the opportunity to grow as individuals while being supported by the other. Over the years, we told the story in these photographs with this simple phrase: "You don't have to be in the same boat to journey together." A mantra that has worked well for us, twenty years and counting.

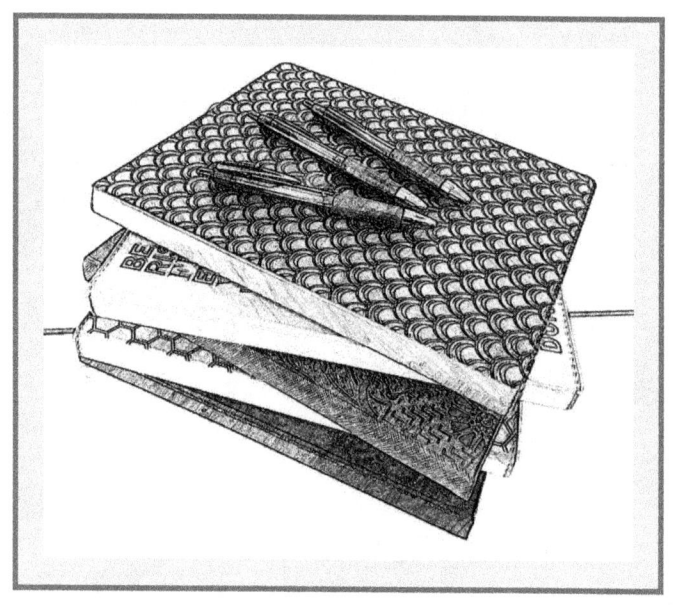

Morning Pages are three pages of longhand, stream of consciousness writing, ideally done first thing in the morning.

♦ Julia Cameron, *The Artist's Way*

6

Morning Pages

◆ ◆ ◆

LIGHT FILTERED THROUGH THE BEDROOM BLINDS. Morning arrived, once again. Another long day stretched ahead. A day with too many hours to fill, too much emptiness to live. I sighed into the sheets. How I wanted to remain in bed to sleep away the hounding questions that kept nagging me. My restlessness had not quieted since moving into Simplicity. Without a job, my life felt adrift. I had no purpose to my day. Art, sadly, felt like a distraction rather than a career fit.

Part of me shouted, *Get up and get going. Do something. You'll feel better.* Wise words, but they formed immovable barriers around taking any action. Able to clean the house, cook meals, and do everyday tasks, everything else was tainted by not having a career, a calling, a purpose.

Do what? I asked the invisible force. My identity as a professional woman was at stake.

Lying in bed, I thought about going for a run. As an athlete, I knew the power of physical activity to help fight depression, make you feel better, change your mood. But I felt no rush. Nothing was on the calendar. *I'll do a run later*, I promised. I turned over in bed, putting my head under the pillow.

Question after question blurted in my head; there

was no hiding from them. *What will you do with your life? What will you do with all that potential within you? What's your worth without a job? What are you afraid of?* These were the questions I heard every morning, the questions that taunted my nighttime dreams, the ones that had no resolution.

I never thought I would be without work. Jobs came my way. In the past, I was sought out, desired, wanted, known for my capabilities and personality. In the move to Wisconsin, I was an unknown, a woman without a job, without connections. Here I was with unemployed talent, limitless time, and unfocused thinking. Where does all that go when not engaged? Mine introduced me to depression.

"What can I do?" Don frequently asked with compassion. As an empathetic partner, I knew he was hurting too.

"Nothing," I responded. "Listening and simply being with me is what I need. I know this questioning is important. Surely the answers will come." I spoke the words with more confidence than I felt.

This scenario repeated itself frequently, over days, over months.

"What can I do?" he'd ask.

"Nothing."

Both of us, helpless.

Don would reiterate my achievements, the ways I make a difference in people's lives, how I show up in the world full of determination and grace. His words tried to penetrate my sadness. Much later he admitted that he wondered who I was during those dark days. I wondered too.

One morning he suggested, "View this as a break from the job market, a sabbatical from work. Find what makes your heart sing."

Oh, how I wanted my heart to sing once again.

I had heard about Julia Cameron and morning pages. Intrigued, I went to Barnes & Noble and bought *The Artist's Way*. The cover promised a course in discovering and recovering your creative self. Would I find her in the suggested twelve weeks? My track record with self-help books began with grand determination, losing interest after thirty pages. I found most contemporary self-help books repetitive and tedious with countless exercises that seemed meaningless. Was my current quest to find myself and my purpose desperate enough to hang in there for 222 pages?

Julia's words brought comfort. She understood about being lost in one's own life. While her despair came from alcoholism and mine from loss of vocation, she was a kindred spirit. I signed the contract in the front of the book, committed to live with the prescribed Artist Way formula of writing morning pages, planning a weekly artist date, and doing the exercises for twelve weeks.

Mornings now began with something to do. I had morning pages to write. Three pages of whatever was on my mind, whatever was hanging in my heart, whatever words came while never letting the pen leave the page. No intention to be brilliant or wise or witty. Don't think, don't plan, don't worry. All the ugly feelings, disappointments, unknowns, and fears were written in a benevolent journal that felt comfortable in my hands. Just looking at the textured red cover invited words. Still, I struggled to write three pages morning after morning. I reminded myself that this was better than facing the redundant questions without answers. While I continued to function by painting and handling the day-to-day household tasks, the relentless question of what to do with my life haunted me. *The Artist Way* was my shield of defense against those penetrating barbs. I had morning pages to write, exercises to do, an artist date to plan.

Months of this morning practice confirmed the value of a sense of order and minimalism. There was a difference in me as I became grounded in discovering myself and who Simplicity was as well. What we placed in Simplicity was just enough and nothing more. This idea of minimalism showed up in how I painted. Simple designs appealed to me, keeping life simple was my mantra, eliminating the extraneous was my favorite challenge. As a child, I kept my room clean and orderly with what was important to me, nothing more. I spent childhood rearranging my room, finding multiple ways to create my world in a small space. This intrigue and partnership with the aspects of simplicity continued throughout the years, wherever and however I lived.

As I faithfully wrote those three pages, morning after morning, the plaguing questions moved from banging in my head onto the page. As they looked up at me, scribbled in pen, they were not as disturbing, serving as gateways to a new part of me. Answers started arriving with different questions joining in. *What is the basic intention of this room? How does clutter make you feel? What is most important about an entrance? How does a room welcome?*

Now I was mind mapping, drawing circles on paper, making connections between this and that. A puzzle was being put together. Questions formed the border and as the answers came, they filled in the picture. I found myself creating a unique business as an artist of space and place. By listening to the rooms of Simplicity and the buildings I entered, I heard their stories. I experienced comfort or awkwardness in how they were used. A lifetime love of spaces was finding a possible vocation. I had no idea how to market this grand and glorious idea, but that was not important. Not now.

Each morning I wrote three pages, followed by a walk. As my body moved, my mind created. Then I was off to do research at the library or Barnes & Noble, interviewing architects and designers, all the while observing how people used and engaged spaces. There was a simple structure to my day. Reminded that the characters in the Chinese word for crisis mean both danger and opportunity, I realized that my crisis had opened an opportunity, had forced me to ask deeper questions of myself. I was discovering my purpose, knowing it partnered with my skills and talents. Now, when the familiar questions arrived, they became the pieces of a puzzle to be explored, not avoided or hidden under the pillow as in the days before.

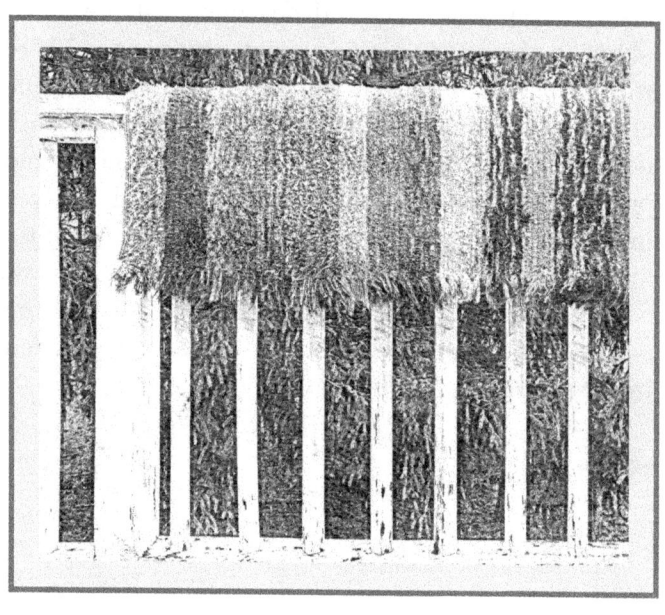

A few days of neglect and the soul goes out of the house.

♦ May Sarton, *Journal of a Solitude*

7

From Work to Caring

◆ ◆ ◆

Having lived in older houses most of my adult life, I can attest they need lots of care. While dusting and vacuuming are a given to any house, with older ones it takes an additional effort. Old houses have extra ridges, angles, and crannies that gather the unwanted. When I clean just to get it done, I resent the time spent. I have noticed that this attitude is often accompanied by a rather bad job of cleaning.

Rather than feeling put out and irritated with floors, sinks, and tops of tables needing regular attention, I changed my philosophy into a mindfulness where I am fully present when I dust or sweep, giving gratitude for a house that provides for us. The reward is knowing the house is clean and that I have honored our living spaces. Both the house and I are happier.

I love to reside in a clean and orderly house. Living in a refreshed house makes what happens there run more smoothly. Like being in a washed car that suddenly drives better. I know many people do not share this kind of due diligence to housekeeping practices. This once included my husband, a serious procrastinator in the cleaning department.

While living in Simplicity, Don and I divided the house chores. He took charge of the bathrooms and the family room in the basement. I was assigned the hardwood floors and rug shaking, as well as dusting. We each cleaned our own offices, and together we tended the kitchen.

We have come a long way in our relationship around house tasks. Don would be the first to admit that cleaning was an imposition, a job to be done. Watching him clean was like observing a mad man, many places untouched by his quick "get it finished" approach. While appreciative of his willingness and sense of mutual responsibility, his way of cleaning put me on edge. Tense conversations and frustrated silences frequented between us, a sore spot that oozed every cleaning day. I nagged. He felt scolded. We agreed the issue had to be addressed. The dust mop and its pathway through the house were not as important as our marriage.

I shared that for me, house care was about respecting Simplicity and each other. I spoke of our house as a home to our hopes and dreams as well as a support for our everyday rhythms. As we talked openly about the mundanity of cleaning, it led to a new understanding of our responsibility to this house. Tasks were ways we loved Simplicity and honored each other's needs in living together. More importantly, the direct conversation about cleaning improved that part of our relationship. Fewer moments of angst. Fewer full-bodied sighs. In the end, Don jumped up his cleaning game, and I relaxed my stringent regulations.

One of the earliest books I remember reading on housecleaning was Sarah Ban Breathnach's *Simple Abundance*. Her words invited me into a different understanding around creating home, giving housecleaning value and honor: "Stop calling your daily round 'housework' and begin to call it 'homecaring.'" By changing the name of housework to homecaring, I experienced a change in my attitude.

There must be quite a few things a hot bath won't cure, but I don't know many of them.

♦ Sylvia Plath, *The Bell Jar*

8

Soaking in the Tub

◆ ◆ ◆

SIMPLICITY WAS A HOUSE WITH UNIQUE FEATURES. She hosted two interior staircases, a hand crank doorbell, and floorboards in the 1905 part of the house that went different directions from the 1925 addition. By far the most noticeable and novel feature was the bathroom on the main floor. This deep narrow space off the living room invited one into a different time, becoming a conversation piece when we had first-time guests. While not original to the house, the remodelers installed a vintage claw foot tub and a European-style water closet that had its tank elevated high above the stool. Flushing happened by pulling a hanging chain. Our young grandchildren found delight and giggled with this added task to the bathroom routine, often needing to stand on the toilet seat to reach the chain.

Both children and adults came under the spell of the claw foot tub. If guests stayed the night, an evening soak before bedtime was frequently indulged. Designed for lounging, the smooth white pearly basin, called a slipper tub, was even asked to smile in its very own photo shoot. Used as the cover for a music CD, the tub was filled with as many rose petals as could be gathered from the local florist. Imagine slipping into that kind of texture and fragrance.

Once this deep, long sloping tub found your body, you were hooked. Mineral salts, candles, books, and music were within reach to transform a bath into a ritual. Here was where thoughts lingered, ideas emerged, and every cell in the body took a long exhale. No need to rush. Time elongated, allowing an opportunity to linger until the water turned cold. As the Roto-Rooter commercial used to say: "Away go troubles down the drain." A lovely detox anytime of the day.

When Don or I was stuck in a creative process or flummoxed by life, time in the tub sorted it out. We emerged from those waters renewed and in a better place. I am in total agreement with Sylvia Plath who seemed to have much to say about the bath. "There must be quite a few things a hot bath won't cure, but I don't know many of them. Whenever I'm sad I'm going to die, or so nervous I can't sleep, or in love with somebody I won't be seeing for a week, I slump down just so far and then I say, I'll go take a hot bath.... Then you lower yourself, inch by inch, till the water's up to your neck. I never feel so much myself as when I'm in a hot bath." Oh, Sylvia, my words exactly.

I have three chairs in my house. One for Solitude, Two for Friendship, Three for Society.

♦ Henry David Thoreau, *Walden*

9

Chair Tales

◆ ◆ ◆

SITTING IS NOT THE ONLY USE OF A CHAIR. Remember putting two chairs back to back then throwing a blanket over them to make a tent? As a child, I sat backwards on a chair, added some rope, and suddenly I had an imaginary ride on my horse named Silver. A dancer I knew choreographed an entire performance using a chair as her partner. We get up on a chair to reach something or to get the attention of a noisy crowd. We also use the word chair as a metaphor to speak of the "chair of the department" and "first chair" in the orchestra. Chairs give us a vantage point from which to see the world as we snuggle into them to read a book or newspaper, share in a conversation, or think out a creative thought. They sit in readiness in the rooms of our homes as willing partners in the sculpting of our everyday lives.

Each chair in Simplicity had a distinctive and artful character with a story to tell. The most dominant of our collection was an independent and strong overstuffed chair with matching ottoman. She was referred to as the Katharine Hepburn chair, specifically purchased for my quaint 1930s bungalow named after my favorite actress. Moved from house to house, this chair maintained a strong presence in any room. The neutral tweed fabric allowed her to be easily partnered with most furniture. She was larger than any other chair in the house, so care was taken as to where she would be positioned in a room. She was accommodating, providing enough room for me to tuck my feet underneath and wiggle my body into just the right place. Sitting in this chair brought comfort and a sense that my world was as it should be. If she could have talked, she would have said:

> *I hold thoughts and emotions well. With plenty of space to snuggle in, I offer room to think. The comfort I provide the body invites a long, lengthy read of a book or time to journal complete with pauses. No hurry to get up. Just be.*

A stately wooden Windsor chair had belonged to my Aunt Dorothy. I loved seeing it in her well-appointed home and delighted in receiving it when she moved to smaller quarters. Its tall back allowed the head to relax, and the arm rests were supportive as they wrapped around the body. At one point, I decided to paint this chair a cranberry red, a bold move as I heard the antique lovers in my head laying on the guilt. I never regretted that decision. It had more spunk and stood out in a pleasant way, rather than quietly retreating into the woodwork as it once did. To invite a more comfortable sit, a pinstriped cushion was added. I giggled that this antique chair was a very trendy cranberry color, sporting a cushion from IKEA. Talk about a personality change! This is what the Windsor chair might have said:

> *I am the extra. Usually chosen last, people prefer the upholstered seating to me. In*

spite of my wooden frame, I am amazingly comfortable. My classic style and new color give aesthetic value to any room, plus, I am the only chair that is easy to move into place. I am the versatile extra that is needed when the room hosts more people, but most of the time I am vacant and waiting.

A curved captain's chair was the only remaining chair from my great-grandmother's dining set, inherited by my parents. The matching chairs of this set were oddly uncomfortable. No matter what size body sat in them, it felt as if you were slipping off, but the captain's chair was special. My father sat in this chair at the head of the table. In seeing it, I felt his energy and love of life. Sitting in it, I returned to my childhood home and family dinners. This was a chair that remembered well:

> *Jim and I were good buddies. He was a grand and glorious storyteller and many of his tales were shared when he sat with me. His sense of humor brought joy and laughter from his audience around the table. Sometimes he would do a magic trick. Once he offered me to a friend of Susan's who had just learned to parachute. Jim pulled me into the middle of the room and said, show me how you jump, and indeed he did.*

Two matching brown tufted chairs were purchased after we moved into Simplicity. Originally for our library, they moved to other places in the house. Most of the time they resided in our living room across from the Katharine Hepburn chair. Usually they were angled to support an easy connection between the people who sat in them. Working best as a team, we rarely separated the pair. A small table sat between them to offer a place for a cup of coffee, a book, or anything that let a conversation be hands-free. Hospitality and comfort were the qualities found in the friendship chairs, and they would have said:

> *We have heard the deepest sorrow and greatest joy by those who sit with us. People sit for quite some time as they unpack life with its ups and downs. There are times of silence, times of tears. Frequently, we witness the trust and support of friends who sit on us.*

One of my favorite stories about chairs came from touring Eleanor Roosevelt's home, Val-Kill. When the docent was asked why Mrs. Roosevelt's living room chairs were so eclectic and unalike, she responded, "Mrs. Roosevelt said her guests were different shapes and sizes, therefore, it was important to have her chairs reflect this as well."

The chairs in Simplicity came in multiple shapes and sizes, colors and textures. Each had a story to tell. Each offered a place to be yourself.

If you are going to create in your kitchen, the room needs to be as conducive to creativity as a painter's loft or a potter's shed. It should be efficient, fit your lifestyle, and lift your spirits when you walk in.

♦ Victoria Moran, *Shelter for the Spirit*

10

Kitchen Wisdom

◆ ◆ ◆

SIMPLICITY'S KITCHEN WON OUR HEARTS THE FIRST day we walked in. Located in the middle of the house, the kitchen stretched the full width of her size. Light entered through the long windows from both the east and west. Her maple wooden floor, beautifully refinished, added charm. Something about those two elements—the windows and floor—felt simple, organic, and joyful.

We entered the house through the kitchen door. As a result, this hub of Simplicity collected elements from our comings and goings. Chaos and overwhelm quickly gathered. While Don and I preferred a clean counter, making that happen was a constant challenge. A block of knives had rental space on one stretch of counter, granted permission because of frequent use. Everything else had a designated place behind a cupboard door, easily accessible, but out of sight.

Because I work best in a kitchen that is orderly and efficient, I have developed several kitchen mantras for myself:

- *As few small electrical appliances as possible.* Because I prefer not to have them on the counter, they require storage space, which was at a premium in Simplicity.

- *Awaken to a clean kitchen.* Don was on deck with this one. An early riser, he brought this room to order, made the coffee, and gifted us a clean canvas of counter space.

- *Everything needs a place.* Two areas of daily clutter in Simplicity's kitchen were the island and the counter closest to the outside door. This was where the randomness of the day landed and quickly accumulated. Constant management was needed to keep papers filed, mail sorted, tools returned to the basement workbench, and dirty dishes put in the dishwasher.

- *Ask questions.* Space was a precious commodity in Simplicity's kitchen and every item had to be worthy enough to take room on a shelf or in a drawer. We asked: Is this item needed?

One day while deep cleaning the kitchen, I asked a question of the innocent spoons and spatulas in my view. *Do two people need all this?* They had overtaken three drawers plus a utensil holder on the counter. I had tried to minimize this assortment of utensils in the past. Each one seemed to have a very specific purpose and begged to claim a place in the drawer. My gaze spotted the Tupperware melon baller. *When were you last used?* Months and years rolled back on the calendar. I vaguely remember using this bright yellow utensil thirty years ago, probably trying to impress with a decorative fruit salad at a church potluck. In looking at this collection of kitchen helpers, I realized I avoided using some utensils. I had my favorites. I had backups. Out went the reserve team. My love of minimalism kicked in. Soon the three drawers and holder on the counter condensed to one large utensil drawer. In the words of organizer Marie Kondo, now both the kitchen and the utensil drawer "sparked joy"!

Perhaps my attraction to rocks was to find the spirit within.

♦ Susan Eaton Mendenhall

11

Rocks

◆ ◆ ◆

I'M UNSURE WHEN MY FASCINATION AROUND ROCKS began. Perhaps vacations at the lake as a child. Sometimes the color caught my eye. Sometimes the shape made me pick it up. How it felt in my hand could be the invitation for one to join my beloved rock family.

Rocks adorned Simplicity on window ledges, in pottery bowls and baskets, and around plants. Fortunately, Don appreciates rocks as well. On a trip to England, independent of the other, we were both picking up rocks from our homeland. In Dover, the ancestral home of the Eaton family, I requested time alone to stroll the beaches and sense the rocks beneath my feet. Don stretched out on a bench. He knew this would take time. Finding rocks, being with rocks, was a form of meditation for me. My eyes were glued to the textures and shapes that tantalized my curiosity. My fingers easily fit into the smooth impressions formed into the rock, much like putty. The Dover stones felt familiar, comfortable. Holding each one in my hand reminded me of a place deeply known in my bones. In the English Cotswolds, we picked up a yummy butterscotch-colored stone used in many of the buildings and homes in that part of the country. This is a worker stone, rough and angular. While not a stone you quickly notice by itself, it stands out beautifully in a finished building.

A trip to the Pacific Ocean found me fascinated by rocks that were round, smooth and flat. Again, I spent hours walking the rugged coastline, picking them up and stacking them one on top of the other. I remembered the importance of stacked stones to the Inuit living in the frozen tundra. Called inukshuks, stacked stones have long been a means of communication. In a land of snow and ice, they serve as a marker in finding food and shelter.

Our neighbors across the street had a large inukshuk in their front yard. Intrigued, I asked about its meaning. "We have moved so many times. This place is home. This is where we have decided to raise our children." A variety of sizes, shapes, and kind of rocks were brought from previous places they had lived, found on vacations or in locations filled with memories. Here stood a stack of rocks, an inukshuk in our neighborhood, as a visible reminder of the importance of place, of finding home.

On the southern edge of Lake Superior is a small bay with a unique rock called a concretion. This word comes from the Latin *con*, meaning "together," and *cresco*, "to grow." According to the Wisconsin Geological Survey, these grown-together rocks began forming about 20,000 years ago in Lake Superior. Water pressure and wind erosion helped to create their interesting shapes. To describe a concretion is difficult, as they vary, but most have a smooth appearance with defining lines reminding you of something else. One might look like a round crescent roll while another is very flat with ripples, like on a lake. To the Native Americans in this part of the country, concretions are deeply respected for the wisdom they are believed to hold. Called spirit stones or grandfather rocks, each honors a spirit whose message is gifted to the one who finds it.

Perhaps my attraction to rocks was to find the spirit within. Each holds the mysteries of how it was formed, why it landed in a certain place. When my daughter left for college, I searched for a rock that fit perfectly into the palm of my hand. In giving it to her I said, "If you find yourself homesick, just wrap your fingers around this stone, and know I am with you." Rocks remember. A spirit stone for sure, infused with a mother's love.

The house and I resume old conversations.
   ◆ May Sarton, *Journal of a Solitude*

12

The Conversation

◆ ◆ ◆

Sitting in the Katharine Hepburn chair, legs tucked underneath me, I looked at Simplicity's old walls, doorways, and windows and wondered what she had to tell me. While I felt welcome and safe within her walls, I was not totally sure what she and I expected from each other. Perhaps if I asked, she would make her thoughts known. I was ready for a little chat with this house I was learning to love as a dear friend and confidant.

Simplicity, what do you want me to know about you?

She started without hesitation. Words flew out as if she might not be given another chance to speak. I grabbed a piece of paper, knowing this conversation was important to document. Soon my pen skittered across the page.

> *I am a proud house, nothing fancy, nothing elaborate, just what I am. With simple lines, a sound structure was built. "Uncomplicated with character" would be an accurate description. My simple plainness allows you to create me in so many ways. I am like a blank canvas that receives whatever you paint on me. These old walls of mine invite art. Colors perk*

me up, and furniture moved within my walls adds comfort and interest. Cozy places happen in these boxy rooms. My many windows and doors keep air flowing and are ways to move people and ideas throughout my strong frame. Floors are old and bare, with countless living footsteps having walked on them. Bumps and bruises of my lifetime show up in my worn woodwork. I do not try to hide these as they keep me real. Thank you for seeing me and not being embarrassed. Tall ceilings give you space to expand your living and they make me feel deliciously elegant. Two interior staircases keep you fit and help me stretch my frame. How fortunate I feel to have three porches which allow me to breathe and extend myself to welcome others. Oh, yes, and how I love my new grounding and supportive base. Being moved to this lot meant a new basement for my old bones. I have greater confidence in myself and know I am much stronger. The move was a new beginning for me, just as it was for you. Thank you for loving me into a stately house, a home, once again. May I love you into being too?

Simplicity paused as did my pen. *May I love you into being?* my friend asked.

Simplicity and I understood the nature of each other. We were transplants on this lot, in this neighborhood. She was located down the street, living as a hair salon and rental property. Moving changed not only her location, but her purpose. Standing on this formerly empty lot with no landscaping to soften her, not even grass, she looked intentional and committed. Void of any inside decor, it was as if she had sorted herself out, cleaned off her desk to write a new chapter, emptied herself to be willingly filled with her next story. This was our common story.

I sat in the room with Simplicity and her question. The move into Simplicity coincided with my move into menopause. Sleepless nights, discomfort in my own body, anxiety, and a lackluster feeling were daily companions. Breast pain increased worry about cancer, reminding me of my mother's battle with this disease and death at age fifty-five. I was nearing that number. Fatigue was new to me. Just thinking exhausted me. There was so much to worry about, figure out, work on. My athletic body was adding pounds, clothes were not fitting as they once did. I felt betrayed by my body, by my circumstances, scared that this anxious and exhausted pattern would be my life from now on.

At times, living in Simplicity felt like a prison more than a home. There was a restlessness in the house and this restlessness was me. Who was I since moving here? What was to give me structure where a job once did? I wondered if I should find any job. Would simply being employed make my sense of worthlessness go away? No job equaled no money, equaled no worth. Was that true? Of course not, but I could not convince myself. While my creative energies were finding expression in my paintings, this did not seem enough. This was not all of me. I was lauded by others for my talents, admired for my confidence and independent spirit. What was I doing with any of this? The nagging question of what to do with my life kept me restless. I wondered if Simplicity had felt this way, too, before the move, before she knew herself in a new neighborhood with new owners.

Depression made me feel like a wallflower in my own life, sidelined and fading. My usual energetic nature turned lethargic, finding it difficult to get out of bed or motivated to improve my condition. Any self-confidence I might have had dwindled. Simplicity's spaces spoke to me in metaphors. I felt brokenness looking at the cracks in the ceiling, exhaustion in the worn woodwork, confinement in the boxy American Foursquare rooms, difficulty in the steep climb of the front staircase.

With unmanageable internal chaos, my external world became my project. Years of experience had proven to me that if I wished to strengthen the inside, the outside was a place to begin. I returned to a daily physical practice of running. As my body felt stronger, so did my resolve in living life. I also knew that an organized environment was required to keep me positive and moving forward. Messy drawers and closets diverted attention from the inner struggles into tasks without feelings, nagging voices, failures. How good it felt to accomplish something, anything. I created order out of chaos, drawer by drawer, shelf by shelf, room by room.

I hoped for a home that would help me discover myself. I had to trust that this old house would support my questions, could handle my frustrations, calm my fears, allow my wallowing and indecision, and lovingly hold my depression.

Simplicity did not abandon me.

Her spaces invited ideas, insights, guests who expressed appreciation not only of who Don and I were, but of Simplicity's appeal and uniqueness. Her simple structure and open spirit were invitations to experiment with her rooms. My love of buildings and how they impacted human behavior slowly gave birth to a facility consulting business. In designing my business, I began by asking questions of the public and commercial spaces I entered. The answers were instrumental in better understanding the impact of the space on clients and users. Was it clear where to enter? One business had five front doors with only one unlocked. Frustrating to anyone wanting to enter. Once in the building, did the space indicate what the client was to do next? Was there a receptionist or signage to ensure the client's next step? What in the room developed client confidence about the business? This led to my three intuitive questions asked of the spaces we enter: Do I feel welcome? Do I feel safe? What is expected of me?

While researching the ways environments shape our behaviors, I discovered a field of study called environmental behavior—a combination of my life interests in architecture, psychology, sociology, anthropology, and interior design. If this had been in existence when I was in college, surely this would have been my major. When I discovered that it was offered at the university in my backyard, I applied, was accepted, and graduated with a master's degree. The two years of rigorous academic study were gifts to my hungry curiosity about spaces and human behaviors.

Simplicity's spaces became a palette with which to play and explore theories of spatial relationships. Her rooms and passageways taught me clarity of design, attention to detail, and how to create confidence in moving through a space and through life. I discovered how space opens, invites, and welcomes even those lost like myself. To create intimacy, to feel hugged by a house, was as important in securing trust between Simplicity and me, as it was between Don and me. Although each room of the house was used for different purposes, I experienced how the rooms communicated through harmonious colors and complimentary decor as did my lives as painter, consultant, writer, dancer, and athlete. Each bringing purpose and harmony into my life. As every room of Simplicity had a specific intention, every part of my life was needed to create the full expression of me.

Still cozied into the Katharine Hepburn chair, I felt safe. Certain places in Simplicity were more pleasant to be in than others. Sitting on the side porch, nature refreshed my spirit. Simplicity's kitchen, full of light and tall ceilings, gave me energy. I was reminded of my core values of simplicity, elegance, hospitality, and creativity. These were showing up in Simplicity's decor of artwork and furnishings. The art deco light, pottery, and the Lladro figurine of two nuns were elegant and simple. Her simple structure invited me to be creative, yet minimalistic. The rooms were not cluttered, but intentionally decorated with what was needed and pleasing. In my conversation with Simplicity, I heard her strong voice, the confidence she had in herself. As she spoke, I found more of me showing up.

May I love you into being? Simplicity has asked. I hear the words of May Sarton:

> *I have brought all that I am and all that I came from here, and it is the marriage of all this with an old American house which gives the life here its quality for me. It is a strange marriage and its like does not exist anywhere else on earth . . . and just that has been the adventure.*

The house is at peace. Beauty and order have returned, and always she has left behind a drop of balm, such as a phrase; so her work here is a work of art. There is a mystical rite under the material act of cleaning and tidying, for what is done with love is always more than itself and partakes of the celestial orders.

◆ May Sarton, *Journal of a Solitude*

13

Simplicity's Hospitality

◆ ◆ ◆

"I FEEL SO REJUVENATED AFTER BEING HERE. THERE is a special feeling when you are in Simplicity," said a guest. A friend and frequent overnight guest at Simplicity shared how she experienced her stays in our house. We were sitting across from each other at the dining table, finishing our meal, but not our conversation.

She paused, looked around the room thoughtfully, and then spoke in a reverent voice. "Simplicity feels like a spiritual retreat to me," she said. "Every aspect of Simplicity is loved. Care and thoughtfulness are what this home is about. This comes from the love and respect given to Simplicity and all who come here."

I sat quietly, letting the words tumble from my head to my heart. What beautiful qualities for a home to hold. I thought back to our hopes when we bought this boxy American Foursquare: to create a sacred place for us to incubate our dreams, to bring a sense of sanctuary and safety to those who entered, to offer hospitality and warmth, to have an ordered function in all rooms.

Our friend continued. "Everything in Simplicity has an intention. Nothing is without a purpose."

Simplicity was orderly, not cluttered or overstuffed. Constant diligence was applied to return everything to its place. Her living room, being without a television, was designated for conversation and being with people. The way chairs and tables were arranged supported seeing each other, not a television. While we had them, we did not use overhead lights, preferring the cozy atmosphere that floor and table lamps offer a room. When people walked in, they took a deep breath. Simplicity offered that kind of space. She quieted the chaotic mind, invited a chance to take a break from the overwhelm of life.

I looked around the dining room into the adjoining room. My eyes caught items that were deeply loved and placed with purpose. An English gateleg table from my Aunt Dorothy's home brought interest to a dull and dark corner. Just seeing it reminded me of the charm of her home where everything was placed with loving intention. Nearby, an unusual art deco lamp fit our eclectic decor. I remember the day Don and I saw it in a catalog and instantly said, "This would be perfect for Simplicity." My gaze moved and landed on the black Buddha statue with eyes closed and toes sticking out from under his robe. How carefully I carried him from the gift shop at Frank Lloyd Wright's Taliesin West to bring both a sense of peace and whimsy to Simplicity. Each time we looked at him, he invoked a smile from us. He sat on top of a Japanese medicine chest that came into our lives as a wedding gift. With its many small drawers labeled in gold paint identifying each medicinal herb, the chest itself spoke of intention and purpose.

Don and I loved to have people stay the night. Adjustments were made to Simplicity's spaces so that ease and comfort could be savored by our guests. Rooms were cleaned, bedding freshened, and towels laid out for use. Books of interest to specific guests were placed in the room for light reading before sleep. Robes hung in sight, granting permission to use. If the arrival of our guests was to be after sunset, porch lights and bedroom lamps were turned on to offer a cozy welcome. Candles were placed throughout the house to bring the fragrances of the season. A hazelnut maple scent frequently joined us in the fall. As we entered the holidays, the smells of fir and clove filled the air.

If the guests were our grandchildren, furniture was moved out of certain rooms to give wide berth for the Pack 'N Play and air mattresses. Simplicity's stuffed animals—Ollie Owl and Pete the Penguin and Peaches the Bunny and Molly Moo—came out of the toy box ready to snuggle into children's arms. Nightlights were inserted into the bedroom and hallway outlets to calm the night fears. The refrigerator and pantry were stocked with yogurt, oat squares, applesauce, and grapes. Bottles of wine and beer were put on the shelves for the parents and adult guests. A plentiful supply of sour cream, half and half, and a variety of munchies were on hand for active duty. A menu of the meals was alive in my mind, along with the timing of what needed to go in the oven and when.

Just as I perked up in excitement to receive our guests, it seemed Simplicity did the same. There was a readiness in her, like a lady in waiting. She smiled with her freshly dusted hardwood floors and tabletops, steam-cleaned kitchen and bathroom floors, her scrubbed sinks and tubs—as if she knew that she, too, was hosting. Soon guests would sit in her spaces, sharing their lives and stories. She lovingly extended a quiet hospitality for their stay.

After our guests left, the house slowly found a way back to her everyday existence. There was a general reset to house and home. Air mattresses and sleeping bags were deflated and rolled up. The washing machine and dryer added their support, one load after another of linens, bedding, and towels. Crumbs from the many meals were vacuumed up from under the table, the refrigerator was given a review of what foods remained. The leaves from the stretched dining table were removed, returning it to its everyday size. Furniture found its original location.

With each task of bringing Simplicity back to our everyday ordinary living, I found myself being thoughtful and reflective. These were little acts of care infused with reminders of why we created and shared this space. There was a gracious spirit in this partnership of human and house. There was also an awareness of how flexible and accommodating this old house could be by its ability to expand and shrink its rooms with the activities they held. While moving through the many little details before me, I noticed that I was smiling. I felt no resentment that my time was given to what others might call laborious housework. I was at peace, very present in each simple task. These small details of living life and creating home brought me such delight and joy.

I understood the sentiments of May Sarton in speaking about her home in *Journal of a Solitude*: "The house was at peace. Beauty and order have returned, and always she has left behind a drop of balm, such as a phrase; so her work here is a work of art. There is a mystical rite under the material act of cleaning and tidying, for what is done with love is always more than itself and partakes of the celestial orders."

The house was at peace. Indeed, there was a drop of balm in the rooms of Simplicity.

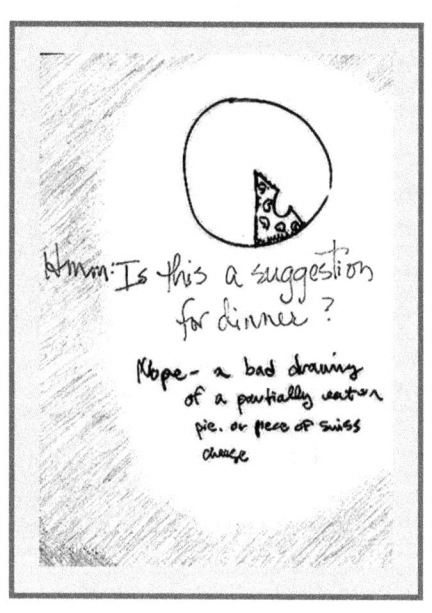

We all know that home has to do with family, the people with whom we live. Indeed, homes comprise people, who together create a place with some expectation of provision, warmth, and security.

◆ Diana Butler Bass, *Grounded*

14

Sharing Space, Sharing Lives

❖ ❖ ❖

WHAT IFS BEGAN TO MULTIPLY. WHAT IF THIS experience destroyed our good relationship? What if we got edgy with each other? What if the children fell down the stairs, became hurt? What if they were unhappy here? What if Don and I could not be ourselves? What if we learned things about each other that were disturbing? What if my mothering got out of hand? What if our hopes and expectations for this arrangement were too optimistic? What if . . . ?

I took a deep breath. What if this situation worked out magnificently?

One of our sons and his family moved in with us. Not long term. They were building a house, and the quick sale of their current home left them scrambling to secure a place to rent. It proved an impossible quest to find a space big enough for a family with two young children—ages three and one—that also allowed a medium-sized dog, could be rented by the month, and was affordable.

"They need us," Don said to me. "We have an answer to their dilemma. We have room. Let's offer them space at Simplicity."

I looked at my introverted husband and could not have loved him more. We extended the invitation through email, allowing them time to think about it. The reasons they might say no made sense to us. We lived forty-five minutes from where they lived their busy lives, went to church, had activities and friends; where they were building their new home; and where our son worked. A long commute might be too much. Perhaps they, too, had apprehensions about living with family. Shortly a response arrived. "That would be wonderful. We are overwhelmed by this generous invitation."

Don and I put our heads together about how our boxy American Foursquare home might handle an additional four people. In my professional work, I knew three factors supported a successful shared space experience: freedom, a sense of ownership, and flexibility. We decided the best solution was to optimize each family's private living space. Don and I moved our bedroom furniture and personal needs from the second floor to the family room in the basement. This allowed the entire upper floor to be home to our new residents.

Simplicity's long-term memory of the second level as an independent apartment quickly returned. Lovingly, we referred to our two homes as the Upper and Lower Apartments. The upper apartment provided each child a separate bedroom, one for the parents, a family living room, a large bathroom with a tub and shower, and laundry facilities. Doors were in place to shut off the two staircases for safety, plus a door that closed off the children's sleeping space from our former bedroom now turned into family room. A further decision was made by the parents to block off the back staircase, using only the front stairs. With a simplified traffic pattern, the family room became the natural entrance into the apartment rather than passing by the children's bedrooms. Drawers, closets, shelves, rooms were vacated and soon held toys, a changing table, others' clothing and personal items. Only a baby crib, dog crate, and their queen-size mattress made the move into Simplicity. The rest of the family's furniture was put into storage. Our new residents had settled in.

Suddenly the spaces of Simplicity were full of changes and new patterns of living. With each family's private living quarters determined, the main floor rooms of the kitchen, dining room, living room, and bath were designated as common space. Don and I merged our two offices into the room off the kitchen, once used as a library and TV room.

Quickly, a morning and evening pattern developed. Our son left early for his commute to work. Our daughter-in-law and the children stayed in the upper apartment until 9 a.m. As the children woke, played, and dressed, they munched on dry cereal in their apartment. This allowed Don and me to maintain our morning ritual of conversation over coffee. At 9 a.m. the footsteps of eager children and Mylie, the dog, were heard coming down the front staircase. After greetings of good morning, hugs and snuggles, the children had breakfast in the kitchen. With our offices located just off the kitchen, a post-breakfast routine found the little ones sitting on our laps talking about life. Inquisitive about what was on our computers, Don found a natural habitat show, and Fridays quickly became Shark Days. I located photographs of the children as babies, doing goofy things, enjoying life. We lovingly held their giggles, curiosity, always asking for more.

Evening meals were often shared. This was the occasion to catch up on each other's day. Frequently, I would invite each one to share by saying, "Let's tell about our day. What did you do today?" Our grandson turned out to be a great conversationalist. Before long, he introduced this part of the dinner conversation by saying, "Let's tell about our day. How was your day, Jazz?" This still brings a smile to my face.

After dinner, the family would go upstairs to their apartment for the evening, enabling them to have their own family time and bedtime routine. Children were given baths and put into pajamas, then down the stairs to give goodnight hugs and kisses. The parents came down for evening snacks from the kitchen, times of conversation with us, and to let the dog out before bed, but otherwise, they settled into their living space on the second floor. We did the same in the Lower Apartment.

To help communication and keep it simple, we hung a large white board on the kitchen wall. Notes were jotted down around grocery needs, tasks to be done, and places people were headed. This seemed to keep the larger family informed and updated without yelling up and down the stairs or requiring an immediate response. Occasionally, the children added artwork to let us know that they, too, had a message to contribute.

"Dog's been fed." Response: "Thanks."

"Rhubarb cobber in the frig—help yourself."

"Off to do errands—back for naps."

"Want to join us for dinner? It's pizza night!"

Tender gestures of love and respect were received during their three-month stay. The porch lights were always on when Don and I returned late at night. This was frequently accompanied with a note on the white board, updating us on any needed information that would ease in our life together. The common spaces of the kitchen, dining room, and living room were picked up each evening of the children's toys. Our kitchen counters and sinks have never been cleaner than when this sweet family lived with us.

We could not have loved this experience more. Everyone desired a positive experience and worked to make that happen. Having the children happy, safe, and feeling this was their home was accomplished, confirmed in hearing our grandson say, "Want to come up to my apartment to play?" Worries that the children would fall down the steep stairs were eased. There were no regrets or damaged relationships. Respect for each other's lives and care of the shared spaces was valued. Just as our hearts grew from this experience, the same was true for Simplicity. Her wealth of rooms and spaces have never been so loved, alive with stories.

I saw the house as becoming my own creation within a traditional frame, in much the same way as a poet pours his vision of life into the traditional form of a sonnet.

♦ May Sarton, *Plant Dreaming Deep*

15

Simplicity's Versatility

♦ ♦ ♦

WHEN OUR FAMILY OF FOUR MOVED IN, Simplicity's versatility became most evident. Who knew her capabilities? Who knew her playful spirit? With each modification, Simplicity found a way to welcome any change of plans. Her adaptable hospitality was to be tested once again. Another family member was coming for a week's visit.

Every room was taken, yet we needed one more bedroom. With thinking caps on, the only space that offered any possibility was the dining room. We moved the dining table and chairs into the neighboring living room. A chair and end table from the living room were added to the soon-to-become bedroom. To offer privacy, curtains were strung on a tension rod and inserted in the wide opening between the two rooms. An air mattress was put into place. Simplicity beamed with the success of her greatest challenge.

For being an old house, Simplicity had amazing flexibility. As our needs and whims changed in the use of rooms, she exhibited a graciousness to this fruit basket upset or Mad Hatter's tea party where things and people moved around. Her simple design was the secret ingredient, allowing an idea to shape a room like putty.

Simplicity's rooms had had multiple lives. The

back room off the kitchen was a tailor's workspace in another life. Prior to that, this room was likely to have been the pantry, as the wall of built-in shelves seemed to indicate. With its proximity to the kitchen, we momentarily thought of it as a dining room. Further consideration said the space was too small, plus I had always longed to have a home library. The space seemed ideal. Not only could this back room hold a wall of books, it provided a place for quieting activities. Having decided not to have a television in the living room, putting a small one here felt perfect, offering just enough space for two people to settle into their comfy upholstered chairs to watch a movie on a cold winter's eve. As Don's photography business acquired several scanners and printers, one the size of a loveseat we called HUGO, the library location was the most likely place to house this necessary equipment. Eventually, the library transformed into Don's office.

What the floorplans called a front bedroom on the second floor, Don and I never considered as a room for sleeping. Almost immediately we named it the pondering room. Our hopes for this room suggested creative thoughts for writing or reading or art, not sleeping. To accommodate our growing love of books, a large bookcase was placed along one wall. The room was pleasant enough, but after a year, we realized we never pondered in the pondering room. Instead it had become an overgrown closet. Around that same time, we drove into Amish country and were reminded of simple living. We returned home and zero-based the room, a process used in my consulting with client spaces.

Zero-basing a room requires taking everything out, including artwork on the walls. When the room is completely empty, the question is asked, "What is the intention of this room, and what is the single most important item to accommodate this?" As Don and I asked this question of the space, one item at a time was moved into place until we became aware that one more piece would overwhelm and alter the intention of the room. The culprit in this case was the oversized bookcase with its many volumes and random knick-knacks, creating too much visual noise to ponder in this small space. As we simplified the room, we simplified and clarified our lives.

One of the busiest rooms of the house was the guest room. Located on the back corner of the second floor, it was the first room accessible by the rear stairs. A door in the upper hallway closed off the suite of bedroom, pondering room, and bathroom, allowing guests to come and go without disturbing or being disturbed. The room was small and simply appointed. A cast-iron bed, found for free alongside a road on Madeline Island, was the signature piece of this room. Guests frequently said their best night's sleep was when visiting Simplicity. We called it the visiting artist room, based on the title of the framed print that hung on the wall. The artwork showed an artist with his paintings set up next to his 1940s automobile. This reminded Don and me that all who came to Simplicity were artists of life. The colors and textures of each guest's life provided a rich canvas of greater insight for our own lives. Every guest was a gift.

Many times I was reminded of Stewart Brand's book *How Buildings Learn*. He documents the many lives of a building after it is built, each occupant making adaptations, changes to suit the owner's intentions. Thinking of a building's capacity to learn makes them feel personable and human—the way we felt about Simplicity. Who expected such cleverness from an old house? With residents who relish moving things around, Simplicity was a willing playmate.

When we keep our spaces simple,
simply beautiful living takes place.

Alexandra Stoddard

Could I be happy in that house? Would poetry come there? How could I know? I couldn't. . . Everything here has been a matter of believing in intangibles, of watching for the signs, of trying to be aware of the unseen presences.

♦ May Sarton, *Plant Dreaming Deep*

16

Dear Artist

◆ ◆ ◆

"Dear Artist," I wrote in my morning pages. "Who are you in me? Where do you come from and where are you taking me? Let me stretch, push, be birthed. Let me be confident, strong, committed." Who was the artist in me, I wondered? What was she to create? Would Simplicity be a supportive place for that part of me to happen?

Remaining faithful to the struggle and opportunity in finding my creative self, lifelong interests were taking shape and form. Since my early teens, unique words and inspiring quotations have caught my attention. Something about a short number of words and the way they are partnered with others creates an exciting discovery for me. Their arrangement wakes me up to see and hear things differently.

> *Art, and artful living, is a constant collaboration between what we are made from and what we wish to make of ourselves.*
> —Julia Cameron

I am a collector of quotations, delighting in finding the next one that introduces me to a new way of thinking or confirms my own ideas communicated in a way that is succinct and powerful. I am forever adding to the collection that was originally kept in a dark green plastic folder. We have been together since junior high. The folder's plastic sleeves hold hand-torn as well as carefully cut out quotations from magazines, newspapers, brochures. Many a found wisdom is quickly jotted on a cafe napkin, the back of a grocery list, shopping receipt, whatever paper is within reach.

> *Do something that inches you toward your calling and you'll probably trigger a great deal of useful information.*
> —Gregg Levoy

This fascination with quotations began with my love of reading. As a child, I would hop on my white Schwinn bike named Lightening, head to the library where I checked out as many books as my bike basket could hold. In the summer months, I found a quiet opening in the bridal wreath shrubbery at the edge of our property. Crawling in with a blanket and books, I entered worlds both like and unlike my own. My imagination had plenty of playmates.

> *Bring yourself uniquely into bloom . . . Don't just weed your garden.*
> —Stephen Paul

The green folder traveled with me to college. There I began adding my own words of wisdom, including first attempts at poetry. Over time, an entourage of self-help books with their wise words inspired and guided me. Post-it notes papered the bathroom mirror, the door, and the computer. Each a reminder to live by these important words.

Often the what in life is not as important as the how or the way we do it.
—Anne Wilson Schaef

In my dark days at Simplicity, the motivating quotations moved from my green notebook into artwork. What did the meaning of these words look like? In what colors? What design spoke to their intention? Abstract and simple became the answer. A palette of colors joined strokes of the paintbrush in creating designs next to the words. This was how my painting expression named JazzArt began, bringing the love of words into a different language. Never a painter before, painting became a new voice, my voice, a gift to be shared with others. Now I needed a place to paint. Simplicity and I had a challenge before us.

A friend once showed me the studio in which he did carpentry and sculpture. He was careful not to call it a shed, he said, because he wanted to work in a place that would foster his art, and a shed is not a place, either in name or design, that nurtures the artistic spirit.

◆ Thomas Moore,
The Re-Enchantment of Everyday Life

17

Studio Space

◆ ◆ ◆

MY PAINTING BEGAN AT OUR DINING ROOM TABLE. Sun entered the room from two sides through wide and tall windows. Painting was a joy in this peaceful space filled with light. Watercolor paintings were soon scattered all over the table as well as the floor while they dried. I had taken over the room. As I became more serious about painting and selling, I desired a more permanent space where I could make a mess and leave it. Putting everything away when a meal was served was tiring. This space in the sun-filled dining room was temporary.

Directly above the dining room was my first office, also called the pondering room. It became my next studio. The light entered differently than in the dining room. The energy seemed off, not as alive and playful as I experienced in the room below. The windows were smaller, the ceilings lower. Painting in this room felt forced, but not seeing another option, I was determined to make it work. Wanting to be supportive, Don acquired a second-hand drafting table for me. We moved it into one of the corners. With care and intention, I set up my paints, brushes, and jars of water. Roommates with my consulting business and the writing of my master's thesis, painting now squeezed into this already small room. At the desk, I wrote reports and documented research. At the drafting table, paints and brushes were in readiness. Frequently, I felt as if the left and right sides of my brain were divided in this room, one in each corner. All waking hours were devoted to my thesis and consulting business. *I will paint when I have more time,* I told myself. Days, months passed. The paints unused, the brushes silent. Nearly unbearable to see them, be in the same room with them, I felt guilty. My good intentions to paint were not materializing. Eventually, I packed up all art supplies, removed the drafting table from the room, and put everything in basement storage. With laser focus I gave my time and attention to school and building my business.

While no longer in view or near at hand, the paints were not far from my yearning heart. I reframed this absence from painting as a pause, not a stop. Someday we would find each other again. Remembering an earlier time when I put my dance life on hold, then returned three years later with bountiful energy and new choreography, my heart was comforted and calmed. May this be so.

Years passed. In conversation with a friend, she mentioned she was taking an online painting class. Not a watercolor class, but one using acrylics and large canvases. As she talked, I realized that I was desperately wanting a new experience to push limits, to discover what was inside of me waiting to be expressed. This was the perfect opportunity to return to painting. In calculating the space required for large canvases, giddiness overcame me. I was about to move beyond a small table and a 5 x 7-inch painting.

Fall weather coincided with my online class. A wild idea also arrived. I hatched a plan, then talked with Don. "What if I made one side of the garage into a studio? And that large shipping crate that your printer Hugo came in, could I have that for my easel?" His excitement in seeing me return to painting was affirmation enough. We set to work. One of the cars would sit in the driveway while I expressed myself in its vacant berth. The large shipping crate easily became a makeshift easel. We added nails to the wall of our old detached garage for additional canvas space. I was ready.

With the open garage, exhilarating autumn air and bountiful natural light filled the space and touched the canvases. My eyes were wide with wonder. Trying to take a deep breath, emotions filled every inch of me with tears ready to fall. Energy as I had never experienced flew in through the open door and graced every brushstroke. The dancer inside of me showed up. Paint moved across the large canvases as did my body. I played. I explored. Every muscle moved and expressed itself.

Then winter came to Wisconsin.

Heating this exterior space was impossible. Giving up this awakened sense of artistic expression was unthinkable. My space demands were greater than what the dining room table and the upstairs office could accommodate. The words of artist Christine Ivers rang true: *Most of the artists I know work at their kitchen tables, in spare bedrooms, in the laundry room, or wherever they can find space to spread out and be messy.* I was not alone in making adjustments in order to have space in which to create artwork. I've always believed that necessity is the mother of invention. That was when I claimed a space in the storage room.

That meant shoving things around, putting up partitions to avoid seeing the fullness of stuff that shared space with me. I pushed, moved, and restacked anything in my path. Don and I hung a gray tarp from floor to ceiling, covering the poured cement wall and visible insulation. The easel made from the shipping crate was hauled from the garage and rested against the wall. The canvases had a home.

My great-grandmother's dining table, stored under the basement steps, was activated for duty. A table full of memories where aunts and uncles gathered for Sunday dinners, games of Michigan Rummy were played, and conversations lingered for hours. I could hear my great-grandmother giggle, see her eyes dancing with glee over this new use of her old table. My watercolors would be very happy with their new home.

Shelving was cleared off for art supplies and paper. The drafting table was set up. In addition to the small basement window, two overhead bulbs were changed into natural light while task lighting was placed on both tables. Light is so important. Would this be enough? As the pieces of the studio came together, I wondered if I would feel creative and happy in my new place. Could this quadrant of the dark basement with its encroaching storage feel welcoming to my creative spirit? Time would tell.

Rarely did I say, *I am going to the basement to paint*. Rather, I gave this creative act a sense of dignity by saying, *I am going to my studio*. It deserved respect, for such incredible happenings occurred there. Transformation of a blank paper or canvas often took me on a journey I had not planned. Something magical happened. A connection to a vulnerable and playful part of me woke up. Watching the paints turn into expressive statements created a peaceful solace unlike any other experience. Without awareness, minutes flew into hours. Empty white canvases transformed into colors full of life.

Naturally, frustrations joined me in the studio.

Exasperations, annoyances, disappointments were my companions. I learned to respect them. Each one taught me something new. While I disliked their nagging and doubting voices, if I stuck with it, pushed into each one, before long an opening appeared. No longer tedious, creating became effortless. There was transcendence in a totally unplanned moment that resulted in a work of art that was worth all the hours and days of frustration. *Do the work. Trust the process.* I heard the voice of my art teacher.

While I felt most fortunate to claim this space in the basement, it was not ideal. I missed natural light, fresh air, outdoor sounds of birds and children at play. I missed the energy and freedom I felt when painting in the garage. But for a moment in time, a corner of the storage room was doing its very best.

"I am going to my studio to paint," I shouted to Don as I descended the steps into the basement and entered the storage room. As I became Jazz the artist, both the space and I were transformed. All I saw were paints and possibility.

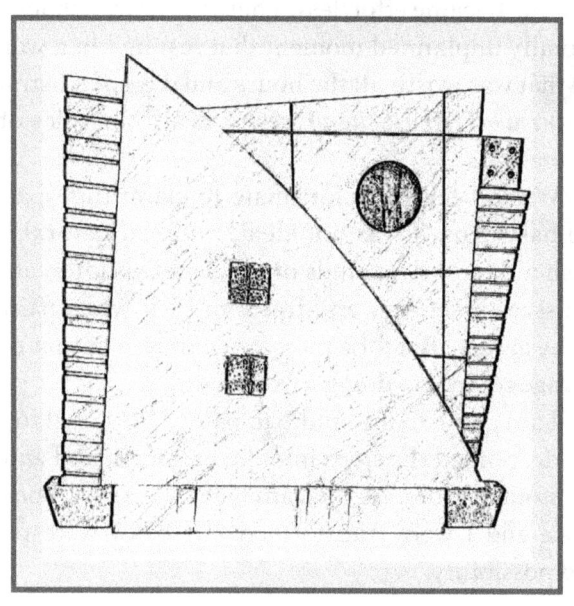

Our surroundings are potentially the most powerful artform we experience in our lives.

♦ Christopher Day, *Places of the Soul*

18

Art on the Walls

◆ ◆ ◆

THE WALLS OF SIMPLICITY WERE FULL OF ART, each painting, photograph, or print intentionally chosen to live there with us. The artwork we selected, ours and that of other artists, had to intrigue us, prompt good questions, tickle our creativity, and keep us interested day after day. Each piece of art was a friend with whom we had conversations about composition and life. Each inspired, comforted, humored, told a part of our story, and increased the enjoyment of living in this old house we called home.

We constantly changed what was on our walls and noticed that Simplicity tolerated those modifications with good spirit. This was how Don and I evaluated our own paintings and photography: we hung a piece on the wall and lived with it. As artists, we posed questions to our work on the wall: *Are you complete? Are you the vision we saw, heard, attempted to interpret? Did we do you justice? Is this where you belong?*

Then we had a new kid on the wall. He arrived in a cardboard sleeve held together by elastic ties. Nothing about this humble beginning made any of the other wall art talk. There was no curiosity or sense that one of them might be replaced. Then, he came out! Unusual colors of turquoise blues, lilac purples, heather greens, soft grays, and a block of orange made their debut. Different from Simplicity's customary warm palette of reds, golds, greens, and browns, this one stood out. Not under glass like much of the artwork on the walls, this was a wooden sculpture, stretching without a framed boundary, exuding confidence in expanded three-dimensional space. This was something the others knew nothing about. They were confined to one-dimensional lives.

When I first saw K-8, the inventory number given by the artist, I found myself entering an imaginary urban setting of contemporary architecture. Oddly shaped skyscrapers rose at angles to each other. K-8's curved arc of wood reminded me of the Sydney Opera House. A round window looked out onto a fictional cityscape. Office buildings and apartments had abstract balconies and supportive beams implied through grooves etched in the wood. A hub of humanity moved before my eyes. Buses rumbled and taxis beeped. Conversations happened in the elevators, coffee shops, and on park benches. The light and dark paint smudges that scattered across K-8 were symbolic of the emotions of people in this invented city.

K 8 hung in the kitchen adjacent to a dear old friend. "Listen, my children, and you shall hear, Of the midnight ride of Paul Revere." These familiar words of Longfellow's poem inspired a painting by artist Grant Wood. Since inheriting *The Midnight Ride* from my parents, this framed print was a backdrop in each of my homes. The multiple shades of green found a calm in me. The earthy colors smelled like the dampness in a deep forest, reminding me of the ravine where I lived as a child. Brown tones warmed the road and made the homes feel cozy.

Not until it hung over the kitchen table in Simplicity

was I to see how light comforted the village. From lamp-lit windows and a moon not in the painting, but certainly there, the light helped tell the story. A babbling brook traveled through the village, a scene I did not notice for years, but now I heard its sounds. The people of the village were like finding Waldo. Where are they? Some were in the road. Others leaned from the windows. The trees and houses were neat and tidy, clean and orderly. The legendary story was transcribed in fine, yet simple, detail.

"This is a painting of a thousand happenings bringing a mythical story to life. Imagine what it would be like to live in that painting," reflected Don one day.

What I know is that each time I walked into Simplicity's kitchen, I delighted in seeing *The Midnight Ride*. The colors enhanced my mood. The tidy houses inspired my painting. The memorized words of poetry invited mine. K-8 spoke in his contemporary voice and suggested courage for new ideas for my own work.

Surrounding us at Simplicity were the known and not so known artists. Each stirred our artistic muse to be brave and take a chance to show up just as these artists did.

What kind of house would support our artistic natures?

◆ Susan Eaton Mendenhall

19

Dream for Artist Space

◆ ◆ ◆

I STILL CAN SEE THE IMAGE SO VIVIDLY. A FARMHOUSE, yellow in color, white trim, two-story with a wraparound porch. From a bird's eye view, two other buildings could be seen—a barn and a smaller structure. A paved road traveled in front of this setting, then required a right turn onto a dirt road that gently curved between the house and barn. The landscape was enhanced by a babbling brook and mature trees.

My heart is warmed as I describe this scene years later. This image came about by request. I asked, inquired, appealed to the wisdom of the universe, the Great Mystery, the Divine, of God. I asked the question, "What kind of house would support our artistic natures?" One night, a yellow house, barn, babbling brook, and a road that curved arrived in a dream. Months later, we bought Simplicity.

Similarities could be found between my dream and Simplicity. She was a soft yellow, two-story house with white trim. Looking at the aerial view with Google Maps, the detached garage could resemble a barn. The front walk curved. The street in front of the house was paved. Mature trees were on the property. No babbling brook, but the bird bath provided water. A case could be made that this was my dream image.

While living in Simplicity, we developed ourselves as artists. Together we crafted the house into a sanctuary for our artistic endeavors. Not only did we each have an office, we had studio space as well. We surrounded ourselves with artwork. Prints of Georgia O'Keeffe, Grant Wood, Picasso, and Rodin were among the famous artists found on our walls. In our travels, we met artists whose work informed and motivated us to explore our own expressions more deeply. They, too, appear on our walls and shelves, offering a delightful diversity of color, style, and shape to Simplicity's living space.

This dream arrived with a set of specific hopes in creating a space for artists beyond ourselves. The barn would provide multiple studio spaces. The outdoors offered a peaceful place to think and renew thoughts. The large kitchen hosted a long trestle table with bench seats, providing enough room for all to eat together. The porch provided a place to relax and be in silence or conversation. In these spaces, artists of all mediums would gather to talk about their day and creative process. A writer would learn from a photographer. A dancer's expression could enhance a painter's canvas. Each person's work informed and added to the artistic experience of all.

This part of the dream materialized in our salon called The Artist Within, which was modeled after the French salons made famous by Gertrude Stein. Creatives like Picasso, Matisse, and Hemingway joined at her residence to have enlightened conversations. Thus far, our focus has been with photographers only. The salons have been held in our living room, our studio space, in a rural B&B, and outside the country on the Isle of Man.

While the image of a barn and babbling brook is not

a physical reality, the essence of this dream is exactly who we are and what we hoped to create. Simplicity provided the space to develop our artistic gifts and welcomed our unique style and expression. Sometimes our hopes and dreams come in disguise, taking years to realize that they happened, just not in the way we thought.

Although it may be unused, the front door continues to appeal to our sense of arrival. Call it the ceremony of coming home.

♦ Akiko Busch, *Geography of Home*

20

A New Door

◆ ◆ ◆

SIMPLICITY NEEDED A NEW FRONT DOOR, A FACE lift requiring sensitivity to Simplicity's age and bone structure. The difficulties of the old door had us grumbling for years. A strong shoulder with a heave-ho spirit was needed to close the oversized heavy wooden entry. Opening was even more cumbersome. Both the deadbolt lock and the doorknob had to be engaged simultaneously, requiring two hands and a great deal of wrist action to convince the locking device to release. Too frequently, Don and I were headed onto the front porch with a cup of coffee and a book, only to stop short of the door and free our hands to engage in this door ritual. While the lack of ease in opening and closing became an irritation and annoyance, the draftiness was a greater issue.

Being that this was the original door circa 1905, it claimed nothing in energy efficiency. No longer tightly aligned with the frame, gaps of light, as well as a slight breeze were evident. While knowing these limitations, we had tried to embrace this beautiful door with its wooden engravings and single pane glass. Focusing on its charm, uniqueness, and authenticity to the house, we had lived with this old door for years. Now the limitations had grabbed our full attention. This was a wasteful, irritating door. Tossing away any guilt about abandoning an antique door, we let our practical minds take on the project by naming the obvious. A door should easily open and close. A door should keep out the cold. And one last niggling matter: We no longer had a key to the lock.

Clear about our task, the challenge was complicated. Not any door would work for Simplicity. Her personality was not flowery or ornate. She was not an oval, hexagon, or full window kind of gal. Nor did halfmoon or stained glass suit her. Engravings with vines or heavy hardware would certainly have overwhelmed her. I feared she would run away if dressed in any one of those lavish and ornamental doors.

Rather than focusing on Simplicity's vintage age, we decided to emphasize the unfussy character of the American Foursquare, a style secure in strong and unadorned lines. Simplicity was a humble house, most confident in showing up with just what was needed and nothing more. Her door needed to do the same.

The perfect match was found in a stately craftsman design. Six small square windows at the top offered just the right amount of unbridled light as well as privacy. The strong lines of the two straight panels below suggested a simple elegance. Despite being a metal door, the dark cherry stain matched the woodwork on the inside of the house and gave warmth to the look of Simplicity's front porch. This door was the ideal fit, bringing Simplicity's interior and exterior into a compatible aesthetic conversation. In addition to ease of use, immediately there was a significant difference in the house temperature, everyday comfort, and lower utility bills.

Everything about this process was transformative, not only in the look of Simplicity, but in our feelings of living here. We became happier occupants. There was joy in easily opening the door. There was confidence that we were secure, warm, and had added beauty to our home.

Simplicity's door welcomed people into our private lives. An old doorbell with a turn-style handle announced strangers and guests, including UPS arrivals where he always added an extra turn. Stepping across the threshold, one was invited into our living space where we shared who we were through artwork, style of furniture, lighting methods, use of colors, and thoughtful attention to how the rooms were arranged.

A front door complements who we are and how we live. Equally important is that each time we entered through this door, we, too, were revitalized and welcomed into our home.

"In our houses, as in our lives, congeniality comes naturally before intimacy." These are the words of Akiko Busch from her book, *Geography of Home*. Perhaps Simplicity's front door was Ms. Congeniality. Just saying that makes me smile.

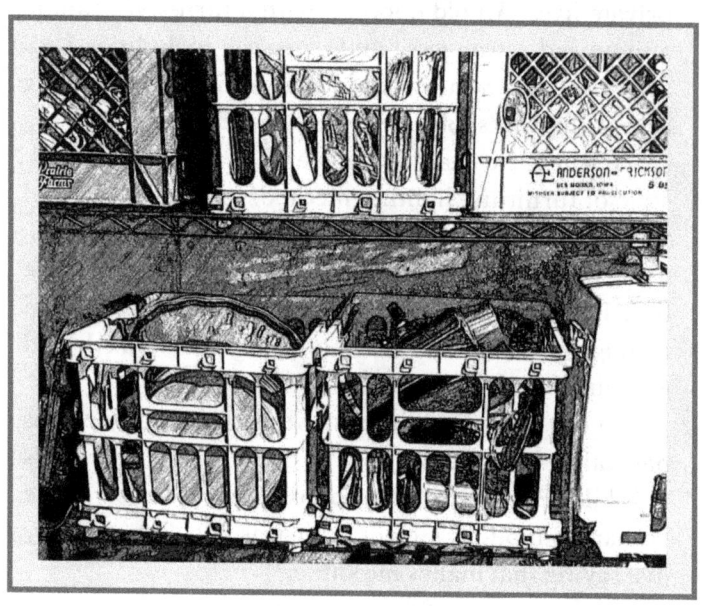

The word "clutter" derives from the Middle English word "clotter," which means to coagulate—and that's about as stuck as you can get.

◆ Karen Kingston, *Clear Your Clutter with Feng Shui*

21

Storage–Where Stuff Lies in Darkness and Indecision

◆ ◆ ◆

THE DESIGNATED TIME ARRIVED. WEEKS BEFORE, we had seen a free weekend on the calendar and promised ourselves that this would be the time to tackle the storage room—a job that required energetic focus. The task itself would produce its own distractions, with the inevitable exit ramps to pause and consider what to do with "this and that." Storage areas are sometimes called the room of indecision. This makes sense to me. Much of what was in our storage area was there because a decision about what to do with it had not been made.

When the day arrived, we resolved to say yes or no, not maybe. Don and I gave each other permission to quit when the emotional overload was too great. At the same time, we vowed not to abandon the project with everything scattered. The goal? To bring order out of chaos. To make decisions about what stayed or went and why. To clean—ridding this part of the basement of cobwebs, dead bugs, and dirt.

The storage room consumed half of our basement. Half of its half housed our studio workspace. The other half, determined by the location of the furnace, had shelving that held infrequently used items like the turkey roaster, movie projector, sewing machine, memorabilia and family artifacts, a filing cabinet with tax and work documents, boxes of other documents with odds and ends thrown in, a workbench with tools, random paint cans, extra flooring and ceiling tiles, and more. Always there was more.

We decided to approach Project Storage in stages. The basics of bringing order, tossing out the obvious, and general cleaning were the focus of stage one. Stage two involved a more involved commitment, which included going through all documents and memory boxes, requiring more strategic decisions and emotional strength than a mind and body can handle in the first run through. Surveying the disheveled room before us, this boundary felt like a gift. Stacked boxes containing material for stage two were shifted to the edge of the storage room. Their substantial consumption of space was a visible reminder of our intentions for another day, another time.

With a cup of coffee in hand, we each took a deep breath, and opened the door into the overwhelming task awaiting us. We had prepared ourselves with empty boxes, trash bags, the Shop Vac, and a camera to document items for Craig's List. Before long we were bringing like items together. All paint supplies landed on the same shelf. Tools were rehung above the workbench. Old boots and running shoes that had landed in a corner were tossed. Improvement was visible. Decisions were quickly being made around what stayed and what went. How many baking dishes were really needed? Two easily moved into the thrift shop box. A butterfly net? To the grandchildren it goes. This was empowering. The Shop Vac made noises as it sucked up known and unknowns—Sounds of instant gratification, making it almost fun to keep going.

Then it happened. Depression and guilt set in as I realized we had not used our tennis rackets in three years, the camping gear had not made it to a state park in quite a while, I couldn't recall the last winter we put on our ice skates, and those beautiful golf clubs—too long ago to remember. A huge sigh came from my suddenly exhausted body.

I took on this closet while Don worked on a different part of the room. Would he feel the same as I in seeing these reminders of a life we once lived? To say we will no longer camp, ice skate, play tennis, or golf felt like a larger question about life, not storage. This needed a heart-felt conversation with Don. I tucked everything back into place, just where I had found it.

Much left the storage room that day. Local thrift shops received our bountiful bags. Craigslist brought new owners and some cash our way. That stack of boxes with old documents? Some were shredded while others were put aside to await further attention. Memory boxes, especially those with family history, remained pretty much as before.

This act of letting go is a constant and vigilant process. With each stage, we dug deeper and perhaps became more honest with ourselves. Hope lived in the items we kept. Holding onto the keyboard meant I still might learn to play, the thirty-cup coffeemaker might host a large gathering, and the camping gear begged for the out-of-doors. More sat awaiting their fate.

Admittedly, because we had the room to store all of this, we did. The good news was that Don and I learned to intentionally bring less into our lives. That changed our approach to buying and provoked thoughtful discussions. Our marriage relationship developed greater ease around what needed to be in our home and why.

Maybe that is the real issue. Relationships. Our stuff holds us in relationship to the past, present, or a hopeful future. Figuring out what goes and what stays is like figuring out life. Complicated.

I found out very soon that the house demanded certain things of me.

◆ May Sarton, *Plant Dreaming Deep*

22

One Thing Leads to Another

◆ ◆ ◆

It's funny about the ebbs and flows of how one feels about a house, a home. One day you are exasperated with all required to live in an old house. The next day you have a small fascination about the way light enters a room, the waves in the wall plaster, the five panel doors. Something happens and suddenly living in the same familiar place is new and rejuvenated. So it was with our days in Simplicity.

The "one thing leads to another" started with the new front door. The door was installed and instantly we felt different. We felt protected from the elements as well as pleased to have provided an inviting entrance for guests and ourselves. But then the satisfaction around the new front door brought dissatisfaction and near disgust at the awful looking curtains hanging nearby. How makeshift they now seemed. They winced, were cumbersome and droopy. Their new neighbor, the stately craftsman style door, had upped the game.

Simplicity deserved window treatments that suited her name. Over the years we had tried mini blinds, curtains of various kinds and lengths, but nothing made Simplicity's windows look happy. Our indecision around window coverings finally came to a clear and perfect solution. Cellular shades were the answer.

Once thinking these too contemporary for an old house, we now saw them as a simplifying update that would enhance the natural woodwork. After the shades were installed, we saw the door and windows as good partners, however, other flaws and inconsistencies were noticed.

The rug in the living room was too demanding. Plus, we wanted more of the natural wood floor to show. We sold the rug, moved the area rug from the dining room into the living room. Did we like the dining room without a rug? That remained to be seen. The room did echo a bit, which was rather annoying. We then decided to move the rug that was in the pondering room upstairs into the dining area; this is the way these two rugs were in our early days of living in Simplicity. Back to the original plan we went.

But then we had no floor covering in the pondering room. We purchased a rug with quiet colors and a simple pattern. It was totally wrong. Every time we entered the room, depression hit. It bored the room. It bored us. Mindful of this negative energy, we returned the rug. We found a replacement that ended up bringing energy and creativity to the space, however, the new rug begged for a different window treatment. Curtains came off the rods, leaving miniblinds and just a bit of valance. Much better. The walls pleaded for art that was colorful and interesting. Photography and paintings that didn't fit in other parts of the house found a home here. The energy from the rug spread and summoned new thoughts and combinations.

Back in the living room, the hand-me-down sofas from my father's house now looked sad. Initially, this sofa and love seat suited Simplicity due to their perfect size and traditional style. With all the upgrades around them, they came to appear dingy and out of place. Don and I listed what we desired from a new sofa: comfortable seating for at least three people, space to lie down to nap or rest, not bulky or too deep, not a sectional, a simple elegance, leather, and well-constructed. We began an active search for what we called the perfect sofa. The first one we saw immediately won Don's heart and matched his sense of Simplicity's new look. He never wavered. While we looked at many more sofas, nothing matched the look and feel of the simple Scandinavian elegance in that rich brown leather. We returned to the furniture store several times to reconsider its place in our old house, sitting on it, lying down, discussing how it would impact the rest of the room. When the sofa arrived at our address, indeed, it was a perfect fit.

But then the walls pouted and expressed their neglect. Had it really been fifteen years since we last painted?

Things, when they are old and beautiful, have a life of their own, but it comes to the surface only when someone 'sees' them again.

♦ May Sarton, *Plant Dreaming Deep*

23

Old House Syndrome

◆ ◆ ◆

SIMPLICITY WAS AN OLD HOUSE, AND MOST OF THE time I valued her charm and vintage qualities. The days I cleaned, I was reminded of how old she really was. Used, worn, and experienced, a 1900s home never felt or looked new. I had resigned myself to the beat-up woodwork. To strip and refinish it—impossible! It would splinter. Painting would take forever. Alas, I did the best I could by sanding necessary places, filling in its gaping flaws, rubbing in a healing wax, and calling it good.

Then there were the old ceilings and walls with hairline cracks and blemishes. We said to ourselves that we loved the character of these old plastered walls. Sheetrock was unknown at the time of Simplicity's birth in 1905. Her walls rippled with age and told stories of another time when walls were plastered over lathe, but the time had come for a professional assessment of the deep-set wrinkles that crossed her aging face.

The first plaster firm arrived with an attitude. When I spoke with the woman by phone, I found her to be pushy and loud. This was also her in-person personality. Not budging from her two steps into the house, she and her husband quickly assessed the living room and said, "Oh, yes. Of course you want this to look nice. We can make your home look brand new."

What an error in judgment. Aghast, I responded, "Look brand new? Oh, no! That is not at all what we are hoping to do here. We love the inconsistencies of these walls. Some of the ceilings and walls need attention, some love and care. Are you able to address that?" They were not interested. When they left, we tossed their business card in the trash, an attempt to rid the house of their negative energy. Certainly, Simplicity's tender heart heard everything, and I apologized for letting insensitive people in her door.

Another professional arrived and we found him to be knowledgeable in the information he shared as well as appreciative of Simplicity's bone structure and facial contours. We learned how her ceilings and walls were constructed—strong and tight. Over the years, and probably from the stress placed on the house when moved to this location, there were a few places where the plaster slowly released from the lathe—a sign of natural aging. This professional was thoughtful and caring, respectful of Simplicity's advanced years. She was past middle age.

After Simplicity and I became friends, I made her a promise: *Simplicity, I promise to maintain your simple structure, honor your age, and respect your strengths.* My words were as simple as that. With each idea Don and I had about changing her shape by knocking out walls, modernizing her character, or adding to her framework, this promise became a plumb line in our decision making. She was an old house. Years of living were tucked into each corner, each timeworn floorboard. Dirt and dust bunnies knew where to hide. While my perfectionist behavior struggled with a clean that did not always sparkle, I learned to care for Simplicity's basic needs while loving her imperfections. As I listened thoughtfully while moving the mop across her aging floors, I could hear her telling stories of long ago when she was young and surely sparkled.

The table is a meeting place, a gathering ground, the source of sustenance and nourishment, festivity, safety, and satisfaction.

> ◆ Laurie Colwin, *More Home Cooking: A Writer Returns to the Kitchen*

24

More Than a Table

◆ ◆ ◆

SINCE FINDING LAURIE COLWIN'S WORDS ABOUT the table, I view this piece of furniture in a different light. No longer do I visualize a table as a flat surface with legs. I see the artistry of its many uses. No longer do I casually set the table for a meal. I create a party, a ritual of gratitude. No longer do I sit at a conference table, thinking only of the business agenda. I consider this an opportunity to collaborate with others. This simple piece of furniture found virtually everywhere creates possibilities and potential where ideas are exchanged, faces interact, and food for both body and mind are consumed.

The space off Simplicity's living room was designated for dining. In the center of the room stood a two-toned table, a natural wood surface complemented by a deep reddish stain on the simply turned legs. While this table extended to accommodate eight people, what I appreciated most was its normal size—a small square. I delighted in a shape that felt intimate and whole for one. My days lived as a single woman found solace at this table. Pushed up against the wall with a small lamp, this was a comforting and welcoming space in my cozy home.

When this table moved into our marriage and Simplicity, Don and I found the square shape was ideal for two diners. My great-grandmother's dining room lamp hung above the table—a scalloped, flower petal design of marbled glass edged with intricate metal filigree. Referred to as a Tiffany design, the lamp created a statement in the room. I remember the many Sunday dinners at my great-grandmother's where focusing on the lamp's details saved me from boredom while the adults talked. Passed down to my parents and then to me, the lamp suited Simplicity. As a signature piece in the dining room, Simplicity wore her Tiffany crown like heirloom jewelry.

Our table was a busy place. At least once a week, Don and I challenged each other to a game of Qwirkle or Scrabble. Suddenly, colorful tiles created designs or words on the tabletop. Eyes scrutinized the opposing partner, next moves were guessed. When the grandchildren came, Story Cubes rolled and created adventures with each picture that found its way on top. Papers and projects had room to spread out, finding both order and breathing space.

Most of our evening meals were eaten there. I carry on a family tradition where gathering for meals is important. Growing up, we ate at the dining table and shared events of the day with a bowl of cereal, sandwiches, or roast beef and potatoes. Manners were inserted into these daily doses of food: ask rather than reach across the table; swallow food before speaking; do not interrupt, wait to speak.

My mother instructed my brothers and me on the proper way to set a table: knife and spoon to the right of the dinner plate, with the fork finding its place on the left. Napkins are to be placed on the lap and used when fingers and mouths were sticky or in the company of food remnants. There is a proper way to hold the silverware, use the knife, return the fork to the plate after a bite. No elbows are to rest on the table. There is a protocol to be followed, and mother, a graduate of finishing school, as it was once called, was the master teacher.

While she was the one in charge of table etiquette, my father delighted in beautifying the table. The extensive tableware options at Chicago's Marshall Field's department store were this man's creative playground. Finding a set of dishes with a pattern of blue flowers on a white background or a geometric design in earth tones would catch his attention and home they would come. He also fancied centerpieces. Flowers from our garden were most frequent. Various vases held a simple arrangement of roses, peonies, or iris, depending upon the growing season. As a child, I remember being intrigued with the heavy, nail-like protrusion that sat at the bottom of the vase to secure the stems. Called a frog, this looked nothing like a frog to me. In the fall, colored corn and oddly shaped gourds decorated the table. Each major holiday was acknowledged in some way. Dad made our home festive. For years, I thought this was the doing of my mother, only to find it continued long after her death.

Each time I set Simplicity's table, I was reminded of my mother's teachings and my father's aesthetics. Eating our meals in the dining room, away from the kitchen, helped to make an everyday happening feel special and intentional. A single candle easily created a centerpiece and focused attention on the meal. Alternating the dinnerware from Aunt Dorothy's red-and-white Spode's Tower with the creamy Wedgewood or contemporary pottery added interest to the table. Each style gifted a different spirit to the meal before us.

Whenever we gathered for a meal, a game, or a project, this table offered nourishment of food and creative ideas, a safe space within which to speak and share thoughts, and the opportunity for joy, laughter, and peace of mind. This was the spirit of Simplicity.

In walking, people become part of their terrain; they meet others; they become custodians of their neighborhoods. In talking, people get to know one another; they find and create their common interests and realize the collective abilities essential to community and democracy.

♦ Ray Oldenburg, *The Great Good Place*

25

Block Party

◆ ◆ ◆

ONCE A YEAR ON A SUNDAY AFTERNOON, THE neighborhood held a block party. Attendance was grand and moods were happy. Salads reigned as that year's popular food of choice—the food of much, the food ever so good. Six chickens—Flopsy, Mopsy, Cottontail, Jennifer, Element, and Moira—who free-ranged with our hosting neighbor, joined in the party. As people arrived, the lawn chairs naturally formed a circle. Conversations easily began with those on the right and left. Soon the conversations darted and dashed across the middle.

Don and I watched the neighborhood children grow up. That year one had just graduated from high school, and he told us of his summer work and college plans for fall. Our youngest neighbor was two years old and captured the delight of all in the circle. As she warmed up to the faces, familiar but not necessarily well known, she giggled with joy. She entertained all our hearts.

A neighbor with a camera problem found a solution in the hands of Don, the photographer. One who had trouble walking was measured for a walking stick by our seventh-grade neighbor who made it from a special tree branch he found. Another neighbor had rhubarb to share. Arrangements were made for the distribution of a dozen eggs from our friendly chickens. The older kids left the circle to swim in the neighbor's pool just two doors down. Wedding and honeymoon photos were shared by our newest neighbors while our oldest neighbors shared that they had just celebrated their sixtieth anniversary by renewing their vows. The neighbor with the annual garage sale announced that this would be the last year, and there was relief in her voice. Another neighbor shared plans about an upcoming camping trip, using our well-loved tent that we passed onto them.

This annual gathering of households brought indescribable joy to my heart. It had not always been that way. For so long I yearned for this connection. After living in the middle of the block for years, I decided it was time for a party. Two families had just moved in, prompting the decision. As we saw neighbors in the yard, we asked of their interest in a gathering. A resounding yes was heard, a date was set, and a party was up and running. An invitation was hand-delivered to each house with the basics: when it was happening and what to bring (two foods, own beverages, and chairs). On a yellow sheet, we requested the names of family members, ages of children, phone and/or e-mail contact information, and the year they had moved into the neighborhood. Our intention was to compile an easy roster to assist in being neighborly and supportive of each other. All ten households contributed without hesitation.

That first year, neighbors came with their rich stories of hobbies, places they had previously lived, why they chose their house, and upcoming events in their lives. Those who had lived in the neighborhood the longest had stories of its earlier days as well as the people who used to live in the houses now well loved by each of us. We discovered each other in a new way that day. No longer were we familiar only by sight. Now each neighbor had a name and a life we better understood. We had resources close at hand—a master gardener, a knifemaker, someone with knowledge of paranormal sites in Wisconsin, artists, a garage sale organizer, a geologist, athletic competitors, someone who knew dog training skills, an owner of a childcare center, and a highway patrol dispatcher—to name a few.

We were a neighborhood rich in the stages of life. Newly married and retired couples, families with young children, families with teenagers, second marriages, a single parent. Each house was architecturally different, just like us. Five houses on one side. Five houses on the other. A wide quiet street played host to our mailboxes. We were a community within the space of one block. Once just neighbors. Then friends.

If I were asked to name the chief benefit of the house, I should say: the house shelters daydreaming, the house protects the dreamer, the house allows one to dream in peace.

♦ Gaston Bachelard, *The Poetics of Space*

26

The Porches

◆ ◆ ◆

Porches are important to a house. They transition into the out of doors. They huddle up against a part of a house and offer shelter from the elements. They invite another kind of living. While there are porches that are enclosed for year-round living, my experience is with seasonal porches.

In my childhood home, there was great eagerness for that day in spring when the porch was prepared for the warm days ahead. This involved washing the floor, putting up the screens, and setting the room for family meals and enjoyment. The door that had been closed all winter was now opened, welcoming a new room into use and activity. I especially remember summer evenings snuggled into a chair, a reading lamp next to me, a book in my lap, the sounds of a summer night as the backdrop.

Simplicity had three open porches. One ran across the entire front of the house, one along the west side of the house, and the third was an open balcony on the second floor. All three had the same white railing, yet each had a specific use and intention. The front porch welcomed our sociable natures. The side porch supported our solitude. The upper porch succumbed to being the best location to shake rugs and dry laundry.

Most of our outdoor living happened on the side porch, located off the kitchen entrance. A hanging swing and a table and chairs distinguished this porch from the others. Private enough, it allowed us to sit in pajamas with a morning cup of coffee or have a quiet meal out of view. Occasionally, walkers going by the house in the mornings waved or nodded an acknowledgment of this woman in her bathrobe. You could almost hear their thoughts. Is it too intrusive to wave? Is this a private moment not to be disturbed?

When Don and I wished to be more sociable, we sat on the front porch. We greeted our neighbors and those who passed by. Conversations easily happened across the yard, the street, the driveway, and frequently, people stopped to chat. They, too, felt more comfortable greeting us when we were on our more public porch.

The porches were where we lived from early spring to late fall. I preferred the side porch because it felt more secluded, private, quiet. It suited my reflective activities like writing and planning. Don preferred the front porch with the activity of the neighborhood. It was not unusual to find us in two separate worlds: Don on the front porch, comfortable in one of our white Adirondack chairs, thinking and jotting down his internal landscape while enjoying the neighborhood activity of people, birds, and squirrels; while I sat on the side porch, writing or sketching at the small round table.

This simple appendage to a house has the power to introduce us to that space between two worlds, of being inside and outside at the same time. Porches bring a sense of calm and rest, as well as the opportunity to think on life. Simplicity's porches physically slowed us down by allowing us to rest in the outside world, and mentally by inviting us to dream, imagine, and remember.

I have wondered how I would have felt about Simplicity if she had not offered these very fine outdoor rooms that extended and expanded our living, our lives. It would not have been the same. Sitting on the porch, I easily transported myself onto a lake or nature preserve. There was a stillness, a peace of mind. The porch was where problems were solved, dreams given wings, and quiet thoughts nurtured. For me, this was where my soul found retreat.

I am not sure that I can grow us an artist until I bring myself to accept that I am one.

♦ Anne Truitt, *Daybook: The Journal of an Artist*

27

Our 10 x 10 Home

◆ ◆ ◆

From June through September, Don and I spent ten to twelve weekends showing and selling our paintings and photography from a white 10 x 10 tent. Before I started this lifestyle, I envisioned it as the gypsy life—spontaneous and carefree. As an art fair attender, I never saw the back side of the tent, only the inviting colors of art and creativity in the front. Once exposed to the other side, I realized that this was a life that required calculation and intention. Every detail was important and necessary. This was a totally different life than our daily living inside the walls of Simplicity.

Much like a turtle, artists carry their home with them. Packed in our trailer were the tent with its zippered sides, display panels and bins, weights for wind, bungee cords, folding chairs, bags of poles, and connecting devices for the panels. The marketing items such as sale bags, business cards, paper towels and glass cleaner, clipboard, sunscreen, bug spray, a fan, stakes for the ground, pens, and sales receipts were stored in a four-drawer cabinet that had its place in the trailer. Inside our vehicle was the protected artwork, personal needs for rain and sun, overnight bags, set-up clothing, show day clothing, and a cooler of food. Every inch of the vehicle and trailer was filled, every item carefully packed and wisely placed to ensure it would not only fit but arrive safely without damage. We lived like artful gypsies. We planned like experienced campers. Both were necessary!

An artist tent is a space designed to display art, conduct sales, and be a store during business hours. The site is likely to be located on grass or asphalt. If trees are present, they add protection from the sun, but may be problematic in windstorms by dropping their branches. Without trees, the hot sun, potential winds and rain are complicating factors both to the artist and the art. A grassy location usually meant uneven footing, adding extra work for the art to hang straight. Each show presented a new adjustment and adventure in living in this fabric home. Maneuvering the trailer onto the site amid other parked vehicles, hoping for enough daylight hours to set up and take down, sore backs and tired muscles, blood blisters from fingers getting caught in the tent poles, and thirty-five-pound weights that land on innocent toes—this lifestyle was in constant motion and jeopardy.

Weather is a primary factor in the enjoyment of this temporary home. Wind, water, heat, cold—all can make the stay miserable. We attempted to keep dry and presentable to the customer; after all, an artist's image is at stake. While the physical comfort of the self is important, ultimately, the safety of the art is the greater concern. Sometimes this means drastic measures such as holding down the flapping tent as it fears to lift off and fly away. Other times it means covering art with plastic to keep it dry from rain or potential drips inside the tent. In the hot sun, a constant vigil keeps moving artwork from direct sunlight.

Over the years we lost two tents in storms. On one

occasion a significant wind shear came through. Our tent pulled up from its weights, somersaulted in the air and returned to the ground looking like a lunar lander. All tent legs were mangled and destroyed. Fortunately, we had not yet hung the artwork. After this experience, we purchased a much sturdier tent that exudes confidence. Heavier weights adorn each tent leg. While much more complicated to set up, the extra time and muscle power required for a sturdy and secure tent was well worth the peace of mind.

This art show business presented some lessons about Don's and my relationship. Both of us are first-born children with a desire to be in charge. Each of us feels that the best way is "my way." We have different approaches to setting up. I can easily multi-task while Don prefers doing a single job at a time. Both methods can work, but not together. For a couple who rarely squabbles, this scenario is fertile ground for outbursts of irritation and grouchiness.

As a result, we worked to find ways to make this life on the road enjoyable and workable. Knowing the "10 x 10 life" is a challenge for the best in any person, we developed two simple rules. Because we did not exhibit in the same show, whoever was showing that weekend was the designated leader. Like the game of tag: You are it! This person made the call on what was what, while the other followed. Before we unpacked, one of us would say out loud, "Remember, let's take our time and be gentle with each other." This was the other simple rule that saved our marriage, maybe even improved it.

Weather, location, and all the parts of the art fair life make for great survival stories, like "I walked ten miles to school in the cold of winter." But the stories heard and shared in the 10 x 10 space make the art and artist come alive. This provisional establishment is a magnet for conversations about the relationship of art and life. While sales are important to keep afloat in this business, the comments from the fairgoers kept our hearts and souls inspired. Where else might you hear how a photograph or painting has touched a life, how it inspired a creative spirit, was a metaphor for living? Our lives were deeply enriched by those who entered this transient home. Don often said "There is no better way to spend time than to talk about art."

Indeed, it is true. Life is explored multi-dimensionally through the lens of art. Spirits are lifted, philosophical questions are asked, ideas are birthed. Art show season dusted off the ho hum of the everyday ordinary life.

Smile: form one's features into a pleasant, friendly or amused expression, with the corners of the mouth turned up.

♦ Concise Oxford English Dictionary

28

A Smile Goes a Long Way

◆ ◆ ◆

I WAS SMILING MORE. I WAS HAPPIER, MORE CONTENT with my life, engaged in creative endeavors that had connections with others. I watched people as I sat in my booth at summer art shows. Walking by, they smiled at me, nodded, came into my white tent to talk about my work, comment on my artist name of Jazz, admire my hat. I realize now, they were returning my smile.

These gestures and overtures to relate bring pleasure and satisfaction. People I do not know, linked only by the artwork, described my paintings as joyful, playful, whimsical, simple, calming. One man purchased a piece because he said it made him happy. He wanted to look at it every day as a reminder. His skeptical wife shared a few weeks later that it was true. She felt it too. That painting brought happiness into their home. I found enjoyment in hearing how my artistic impressions brought joy and meaning to people. It made me smile.

Smiling has not come easily for me. A serious-natured child, I thought more than I smiled. Perhaps I thought too much. Worried over what others thought of me. Worried whether to do this or that. Worry was on my face, not a smile. My mother called it being moody. When I was in the eighth grade (worst year of my life), my mother consoled my self-consciousness at having a large nose, facial acne, a longing to be popular at school, and a discontent with life in general by suggesting I read *How to Win Friends and Influence People* by Dale Carnegie. As I traveled through the pages, I journeyed through my own life, seeing myself differently and others more compassionately. Everyone felt insecure, wanted to be noticed, wanted to be liked.

Hiding out in my bedroom was not an option. I became active in school by trying out for cheerleading, competitive swimming, student council, a talent show, and entering a contest in writing the school song. My smile quotient must have increased, too, although I have no memory of intentionally smiling to get through these days. No one was more surprised than I to be chosen as homecoming queen in my senior year.

The days of personal struggle in Simplicity reminded me of those earlier years when I had to get outside myself. Make a move in a positive direction, take a bold step forward, interact with people. In Simplicity I was often alone. Don was working and on the road. Day after day I sat sequestered in the house with my dreary redundant stories, self-doubts, and unanswered questions. Aghast at seeing my dismal and intense face when passing a mirror or reflection in a window, I knew I needed to address myself once again, my understanding of who I was, who I wanted to be. This began by smiling.

I practiced. I had forgotten how to smile. Awkward at first, feeling phony and insincere, I practiced in front of the bathroom mirror. Seeing an upturned mouth did soften my serious face, but my eyes were not playing this game. They could not betray my sad and pensive heart. Still, I practiced. Three times a day, after brushing my teeth, I would smile. I smiled at lamps, walls, at nothing in particular and everything in general. I introduced myself by speaking out loud in Simplicity's rooms and staircases. "Hello. My name is Susan." It felt different with a smile on my face. On occasion I would walk by a mirror and take notice. Surprised by what I saw, I would ask, "Who is that smiling at me?" And then I would recognize her, know her well, yet see myself anew through the eyes of another.

The qualities I wished to be known for as Grandmother Jazz: Storyteller, Listener, Maker of Magic, Celebrating Family, Inviting Wonder

♦ Susan Eaton Mendenhall

29

Becoming a Grandparent House

♦ ♦ ♦

ONE OF THE ROLES SIMPLICITY HAD THE privilege of playing was that of a grandparent house to a blended family of eight grandchildren. No longer did any live nearby, so when they visited, it was extra special. The older grandchildren found their own ways of snuggling into Simplicity by taking a lavish soak in the tub or a long sit on the porch swing, but I worried that the younger ones might forget this house that loved them and got excited when they visited. More importantly, I feared they would forget us.

In talking about Simplicity as a grandparent house, Don and I remembered delight in visiting our own grandparents. So different in style from our family homes, their houses were filled not only with love but new places to play and explore.

For Don, visiting his grandparents' farm was a highlight. The two-story frame house offered more spaces to investigate than the ranch style of his family home. A large porch with its wide railing was a most wonderful place to sit and play. One room, off the stairs, held unusual treasures like ostrich feathers and fragile Baroque figurines. The tool shed, the boot room, the balcony were all places of adventure. This was the house that reminded him of Simplicity.

My widowed grandmother lived in a red brick multistoried apartment building that hugged the front lawn in a U-shape. As a child, I thought it was a magical place, just as she was. The front door of the building led into a small lobby where either an elevator or stairs took you to the upper floors where my grandmother lived. I rarely took the stairs, preferring to push the large round gold buttons on the elevator panel. Once off the elevator I passed several dark brown doors until I found my grandmother's, where her name was inserted into a small rectangular brass holder. Inside, a single room served as a living area and bedroom. Adjoining was a galley kitchen, with a dining space for no more than two people. A window with white ruffled curtains overlooked the front lawn and sidewalk. Today this would be referred to as an efficiency. Everything within reach, compact, and enough. Much like "Goldilocks and the Three Bears," this home was just the right size for a little girl. I dreamed of living in such a place when I grew up.

Many objects in the apartment intrigued me, particularly the telephone. Much older than the one at our house, hers was matte black with a rotary dial that made a loud clicking sound when you dialed the numbers. The receiver hugged the entire ear. The mouthpiece cupped to easily catch the voice. When I spoke on this phone, I felt important and very grown up.

What would our grandchildren remember about Simplicity? Don and I wondered. What would they look forward to seeing and doing when they visited? What would they reminisce about in years to come?

We devised a plan. Don would take them on a field trip of Simplicity's off-limit places, off-limits for child safety reasons. At their next visit, Grandpa Don asked if they would like to see Simplicity's secret places. Eyes lit up. Smiles grew from ear-to-ear. Bodies began jumping up and down. Each was given a flashlight, and off they went with their most capable guide. Up the back stairs to the third-floor unfinished attic where Simplicity's wooden bones were exposed. Down to the basement where a hidden staircase came out through a closed door in the living room. With furniture placed in front, this door was totally unnoticed to our explorers until then. More wide eyes and mouths opened without a sound. Next, they traveled to the upper outdoor balcony where they could survey the neighborhood, peer into the dense branches of the pine trees and onto the roof of the garage. Eager for more, they soon wiggled into the storage spaces under the front and back stairs. There they saw ice skates, camping gear, golf clubs, bins, and boxes. Each location welcomed our eager adventurers, eyes full of treasured delight.

To add to the fun, I, known as Jazz to my grandchildren, decided to write stories about Simplicity. This included telling tales of the porch swing, favorite stuffed animals, the wall clock in the living room, the claw foot tub, the mailbox at the end of the drive, the turn-style doorbell at the front door, new toys awaiting the grandchildren's return, the two staircases and more. Each story was to remind them that this, too, was their place, their home. A total of forty-four short stories and accompanying photographs were sent in the mail from Wisconsin to Nebraska.

Here is a sampling:

BRRRRRRing...

Do you know what this is?
Do you know where to find it?
Do you know how it works?

Of course, you do!!
This is Simplicity's doorbell.
Remember how you turn the handle?

Pretend you are standing at our front door.
Put your hand on the bell.
Give it a few turns.
Brrrrrrrring

Hello!!!! We are so glad you are here!

We've Got Mail

Jazz loves mail. She really, really, really loves mail! Grandpa Don likes mail, too, but not as much as Jazz. She hears the mail truck long before she can see it. "What will be in today's mail," she asks herself? Some mail comes to Simplicity with window envelopes. Some mail comes to Simplicity with our names typed on the envelope. Some mail comes to Simplicity with our names written by hand. This is the best mail because it means someone special is thinking of us. Sometimes we find a letter in our mailbox from you. That makes it an extra special day at Simplicity! Our mailbox has a red flag that we put up when we have a letter ready to go to the post office. Today our red flag is UP because this letter is ready to come to you. Soon it will be in your mailbox. Do you like mail, too?

Friends

Molly Moo and Ollie Owl invited Peaches, their new bunny friend, for a play date. Peaches was so excited! Molly Moo and Ollie Owl decided that a perfect place for their first play date was the swing on the porch. All three jumped on ready to have fun. BUT, the swing didn't move. This was not fun! Since Molly Moo had the biggest voice, she MOOOOOed to get Jazz's attention. "Will you push us, Jazz?" she asked. Then all three sad faces turned into smiles and laughter. Molly Moo told Peaches about playing with you and how much fun they had. Ollie Owl told Peaches about the time you put him in the secret compartment of the living room clock for hide and seek. Ollie was so glad when you came back for a visit and opened the door. That was a very long time to hide! Peaches cannot wait to meet you. He wants you to know that he is very happy at Simplicity with his new friends!

While I know much of Simplicity's life story, I am unclear whether she ever hugged grandchildren. She certainly exuded marvelous "grand" qualities by entertaining her young explorers, providing steps and stairs for adventure, corners for play, and spaces for stories to be shared.

Stairs go up. Stairs go down. They take us places from top to ground.

♦ Susan Eaton Mendenhall

30

Going Up Going Down

♦ ♦ ♦

SIMPLICITY HAD TWO INTERIOR STAIRCASES WITH very different personalities. Both were crucial to the workings of our everyday lives. The front stairs moved us from the living room up to our bedroom suite and the entire second floor. The back stairs were accessed from the kitchen or the back door on the main floor, taking you to the family room in the basement or the other end of the second-floor rooms.

The two staircases also brought up a common point of confusion at Simplicity. Guests often became lost. The culprit was not only the two staircases, but the number of doors. Simplicity had so many doors. Uncertain which door leads to where, our guests often found themselves in a muddle, in a place they had not planned to go. Quite honestly, this bewilderment happened with Don and me. Hunting to find one another was not an uncommon situation. The staircases were to blame.

Of the two staircases, the front was more formal. It was located through a single French door off the living room, carpeted with a classic-style floral runner. A steep climb of fourteen steps led to our bedroom suite. With a window at the top and bottom, sunshine filled this enclosed space. On the long expansive inside wall were framed photographs of our grandchildren. In those, Don had beautifully caught the essence of each personality, seeing beyond the smiling faces into their tender hearts. From the oldest to youngest, we marveled at how quickly they had grown, wondered what they were learning about life, and missed their presence in our home. Taking the front steps easily activated my heart, offering prayers of love as I passed by each photo.

The back steps opened into a distinctive pathway. With the front of the house twenty years older than the addition at the back, this was certainly a staircase of convenience. When we first looked at the house, the information sheet indicated the second floor as a possible mother-in-law's space. Previously, this space was used as a rental apartment with a separate outdoor entrance to its own staircase. Once we moved in, it hosted a master suite, an office, a guest room, laundry, and bathroom. Just naming that number of separate rooms makes me realize that my fascination with tiny houses will likely never be a living reality. At best, I will continue to live with the challenge to simplify and minimize.

I found traveling the back stairs most pleasurable. After walking up six steps, two small landings invited a rest. The window at this halfway point brought sunlight and a fresh breeze on warm days. How I fantasized about having more room on this landing, a place to sit and pause, but the space allowed only a brief stop to gaze out on the backyard and garden. The final six steps entered the upper hallway, the artery to the second-story rooms.

The grandchildren found the two staircases a fun place to play. Going up one set of stairs and coming down the other brought them into different places in the house. A great hide-and-seek strategy. Toys, puppets, and stuffed animals joined them on the steps and landings. Through their eyes I discovered staircases as a playground for adventure, not just a way to go from place to place.

Stairs go up Stairs go down
Stairs go places Destination bound.
Some have landings to pause and wait
Where was I going? Will I be late?
If I sit here, I could play
With toys and blankets most of the day.
Stairs go up Stairs go down
Walked in barefoot or wearing a crown.
Some stairs have windows or photos nearby
of children smiling, saying hi
Others offer a space to rest
To wonder, imagine, be your best.
Stairs go up Stairs go down
They take us places
From top to ground.

On any given day, it was quite easy for me to never run into Don who was also working from home. With my office on the second floor and Don's on the first floor, I could easily bypass him using the back stairs when heading to the painting studio in the basement. This led us to send text messages and emails when we were too lazy to walk the stairs to find the other. Alas, the stairs were part of living at Simplicity, going up and going down, getting lost and being found.

We want a home where we can relax, create, be with those we love the most, and be alone with ourselves. We want a place where we can process the events of life as a whole, a place where we feel valued, useful, and protected.

♦ Victoria Moran, *Shelter for the Spirit*

31

Twice a Day

◆ ◆ ◆

I SEE DON TWICE A DAY. IN TRUTH, I SEE HIM MANY more times, however, the twice-a-day encounters include coffee and wine. For much of our married life, and certainly since we both retired from our consulting work to live as artists, we have created two important pauses in our twenty-four hours. The day begins with coffee and ends with wine—simple pauses that have become daily rituals. Without these beverage bookends, our lives feel incomplete and unfocused.

Don is an early riser. I am not. We laugh that he puts in a full day's work by the time I show up for morning coffee. While I sleep, he watches several documentaries, listens to the world news, solves a photographic issue, and makes headway on his to-do list. I prefer to enter the day slowly. Too early to face the disturbing world news, I write for half an hour while still in bed. Handwritten morning pages continue to sort out my mind while I view the natural world from the bedroom window. Soon the enticing smells of rich, dark coffee find their way from the kitchen to our upstairs bedroom. I am so grateful Don has chosen to take on this task that begins our day together. Having developed a formula that makes the best savory cup, he is the coffee Grand Master.

Choosing a coffee mug is one of the morning

pleasures. Will it be the pottery blue one with glaze that drips and puddles on the inside or the tall one with blue and gray etchings or the white one with a simple sketch of a dancer on the side? The mood of the day easily changes the selection. Which mug best partners with creativity or planning or play? With dark coffee and a splash of cream, our conversations lay out the day's agenda. Who is doing what and where? Should we go into Madison together or do our schedules dictate separate cars today? Is this a day we need to be mindful of both giving time to a mutual task, like cleaning the house or grocery shopping? What's the menu for lunch and dinner? Does something need to be pulled from the freezer or purchased while we are out?

Morning coffee is often a recounting of our dreams from the night before. Don is frequently losing something, like the car or his keys, or getting lost in an airport. Why? we ask each other. What does this mean about his life, our life? My dreams focus around people and relationships. Why did I dream about a person so deep in my past or a stranger who became a central character? What brings them to mind? Dreams provide curious conversation for our mornings as does our response to the current local, global, and political events.

While living at Simplicity, coffee happened in the living room. Sitting across from each other in comfy chairs, I would tuck my legs underneath me. There was a gracious patience to our conversation, a give and take, an awareness of when talking too much as well as the phrasing of a thoughtful question. I never felt this ritual was rushed or abandoned by the demands of the day. This was a priority.

Just as the mornings bring us together, four o'clock in the afternoon brings closure to our working day. Red wine is poured and a tempo of letting go begins. During the warm weather months while living at Simplicity, wine time happened on the front porch. There we caught sight of neighbors out in their yards or returning home, dog walkers, and joggers. Everything within us paused. The day's creative work that experienced both frustration and accomplishment was done. "I feel like I am going nowhere with this painting. Every day I struggle, try something new, add or subtract from the design. That counts, doesn't it? Just showing up every day?" I would say to Don. My kind and wise husband would smile as his eyes said all was well. No words were needed. I knew that the benefits of being faithful to the practice would find their way onto the paper or canvas. He knew that too. Saying it aloud to someone who lived this same quandary was enough. More than enough. We caught up with the other on what we learned during our day while writing, taking photographs, or painting. Insights and breakthroughs found a voice. Recounting the day's travel in mind, body, and spirit brought both peace and accountability. We had worked hard. While talking and sipping, we were reminded that our days made sense and offered value.

These later years of life provide an opportunity to pause. The days of childcare and nine-to-five jobs are gone. Life has a different rhythm. Morning coffee, taken on the run in our earlier lives, is now savored in place. The networking events with a glass of wine are no more. Slowly sipped, the coffee and wine accompany thoughts both distant and near. These are the stilled moments that prompt dreams of narrow boating on the English canals, a new portfolio in paint or photography, the perfect phrase for a story. The moments when a full hearted *I love you* breaks the rich silences and sits with us like a new lover. There is a preciousness to these times together where the pause is honored and we feel blessed.

In chasing dirt, in papering, decorating, tidying we are not governed by anxiety to escape disease, but are positively re-ordering our environment, making it conform to an idea.

♦ Mary Douglas, *Home*

32

Check List

◆ ◆ ◆

There were times when living in Simplicity when a nagging list of involved tasks and chores had to be given dutiful attention. Tasks that had been on the list for years were ready to be crossed off. The indecision about this or that, should we or shouldn't we, was gone. Eager energies to deep clean and update Simplicity were itching to get out.

For us, house maintenance was a bit like boot camp. Don and I would jump into old clothes and special tools would come out of hiding. The to-do list was always growing: paint interior walls, refresh porches, wash windows, and sand floors. In the middle of any one of the projects, we would wane in enthusiasm, ask ourselves why we thought we needed to do this now, and then realize that it was easier to finish than to put everything away and live with the failed attempt. In the end, we were exhausted, every ounce of mental and physical energy expended, but smiles stretched across our faces. We would say to each other, *We did it* and then exchange a high five. There were no regrets, only sore muscles. And Simplicity looked divine with her teeth whitened and skin exfoliated.

Having a deadline was motivating, like having several rounds of company coming or an upcoming art show schedule that would redirect our time and energy. Another motivator was that celebratory feeling of striking the completed task off the list. Whether a check mark, a line drawn through, or something erased from a white board, the sweet reward was that it was gone from the list, gone from the ruminations of the mind.

One year we planted four new shrubs. What an amazing difference they made in our view from the side porch. The removal of a large tree a few years before had left such a gap. The shrubs added interest as well as filled a void. Then came focused concentration on the tight community of hosta plants. Oh, so many hostas. Divided. Replanted. With more space, each one was breathing better. Flower beds were cleared of their winter coverings, allowing spring shoots to see the sun and be encouraged to show up. Cedar mulch surrounded them. Leaves were raked off the raised bed garden and organic soil was added. All back-breaking work, but such a sense of accomplishment when it was done.

Relocating a kitchen outlet required expert help. This little bugaboo had been an irritation since we bought the house sixteen years before. The existing outlet caused the stove to stick out from the wall. A new outlet meant the stove would be in alignment with the kitchen counters. Quite sure no one else would notice, but for me, all would be right with the world. Our handy electricians also installed new ceiling fans. Another household update that had been on the list for too long. One of the existing fans only ran on high, another wobbled, and a third dropped too far down into the room.

Every so many years the porches needed painting. Daunting with one porch, let alone three. Patching, priming, and painting were on the list. The tools were out, supplies purchased, the work started and would finish—as long as the weather forecast cooperated.

Paper shredding was Don's department since it related to the papers, files, and documents he had brought into the marriage almost nineteen years before. Years of putting this task on the back burner caught up with him. Not sure just what moved the switch from pause to full steam ahead, but he was ruthless and determined. Bins, boxes, and bags were finally empty as he was taking advantage of the free shredding services being offered in the village on several spring Saturdays.

One year, in the midst of these household tasks, I dove into the latest Deborah Crombie mystery. At the end of the last book, Ms. Crombie left her readers in the lurch. As my muscles and back took time to relax, my mind entered her complex mystery. By the end, unresolved situations were given closure. Her characters would be starting a new day in the next mystery. Much like the recent tasks at Simplicity, bringing closure was such a satisfying feeling. We, too, were about to enter a new day and most probably start a new check list.

Any definition of home today must consider how new attitudes and values come up against the familiar; how our needs are served by what we know, as well as by what we remember.

♦ Akiko Busch, *Geography of Home*

33

Time to Leave?

◆ ◆ ◆

THE QUESTION STARTED TO COME UP OFTEN. WAS it time to leave Simplicity? The question was not posed for the reasons many at our age are moving into smaller places. Not because we didn't love living there. Not because the old house took work. These were not the reasons this question kept revisiting. The nudge to leave came from our wondering if a change in our living conditions would refresh our creativity.

Another setting could lead to a new life, new opportunities, new learnings. This had been true for many artists over the centuries. Two came to mind. Picasso moved around. In each place he lived, he picked up a different method or color sense or change of focus. Each place helped him develop his artistic voice. Georgia O'Keeffe found her new self and totally different subject matter in New Mexico. New York had drained her creative energy.

Don said, "We are too comfortable, too content living in Simplicity. Our patterns are too familiar." I understood. Was this contentment lulling us to sleep while we desired to wake up? We were not thinking far or wide in this possible move. Our desire was a different residence in this same geographical area that would give us more flexibility in how we engaged and created in our space, how we lived our lives. Simplicity was a house of many small rooms, which had its own charm. But there was a readiness for openness, undefined space, and lots of light.

While I say this change of residence was not related to our age, we still wished to be wise and responsible. One floor. One story. We talked about the fact that when one of us dies, the other has no intention of staying in Simplicity. She had been a house of togetherness, a house filled with the stories of integrating our lives and finding a common path. Death of one would bring a difficult adjustment. Neither of us wished to leave Simplicity in a shroud of sorrow.

Over the years in Simplicity, this "time to leave" question had been given serious discussion five times. Our realtor had been patient as we tried to proactively navigate the what next, where next. We spent weekends visiting open houses, touring apartments, condos, and new construction. Each burst of this search resulted in coming back to Simplicity, feeling loved and supported by this old house. We looked, yearned, imagined, wrote our list of desired features for our new living and working space. Simplicity was up to speed if a quick sale would be in her near future. She was of sound structure and looked great.

We continued to prepare by minimizing our load, letting go. We had clarity of what would go with us and what would be left behind. What had suited and shaped our lives in Simplicity would likely not fit our new home. When we found our next home, we wanted to be ready.

Simplicity gave us energy, invited the creative spirit, and nurtured our love for each other. Our next home would do the same. Simplicity, an understanding partner in this process, was a wise old house. Perhaps she was the one kicking us out, pushing us into what would be another chapter of life. I would not put it past her.

It only makes sense to ensure that our rooms cue the kinds of thoughts and feelings that help us to be happy and productive.

♦ Winifred Gallagher, *House Thinking*

34

Moving Furniture

◆ ◆ ◆

MAKING CHANGES IN MY HOME ENVIRONMENT IS something I am constantly doing, from switching up my bedroom as a child, to later shifting the furniture in our living room. A friend once commented that I was not one who required travel to rejuvenate my life. This was accomplished by simply changing my living space. I do love travel, but there was truth to my friend's statement.

Many people dislike change, especially in their homes. While I understand and deeply appreciate the confidence and comfort of familiar spaces, I tire of the same old arrangement. A stale space affects my mood. Restlessness and dreariness set in. By moving things around, I gain energy.

Over the years, Don became an active participant in this fruit basket upset. Rarely the one to suggest this indoor activity, he resigned himself to the inevitable. As he added his muscle to save my aching back, before long he was offering great suggestions. He does have a knack for this. Such was the case one Sunday afternoon.

Simplicity's living room had several challenges for furniture arrangement. Boxy in nature, furniture placement often felt squared off and constrictive. Six doorways opened into the room. Each one of these entrances provided a necessary and well used traffic pattern. Bathroom, kitchen, dining room, front door, and stairs to the second floor were working entry points. The extra door to the basement was not needed so we blocked it with furniture. All this said, moving the pieces of our living space was always a creative act that involved some degree of frustration.

On this particular Sunday afternoon, Don and I had committed ourselves to finding a new arrangement for our living room. As we shoved chairs and tables, it became obvious that we had too much in the space. What was the culprit? I remembered this same issue when our son and family lived with us. Our daughter-in-law sat with me in this very room as we were about to move our furniture around. Her clarifying designer mind quickly assessed our problem as a large antique baker's table. While it added interest to the room, everything else had to work around it. Once we removed it from the space, life was easier. She and I started placing the sofa and chairs at angles. Quickly this new arrangement brought energy to the room and a noticeable peace to my restlessness.

The new culprit was a brown upholstered chair. Once removed, every other item found a place to be. A small round table came up from the basement, replacing a square table that moved into Don's office. A gold lamp left the room, while a silver one from the bedroom took its place. The sofa hugged the corner and traded spaces with a chair and table. Like wooden building blocks, furniture and accessories moved into new arrangements. The frustrating frowns on our faces changed into accomplished smiles. We could feel the difference. The room opened, felt bigger, less congested, looked happier. Each addition or subtraction of furniture brought a fresh viewpoint. Gone was the commonplace and same old routine. The room woke up and so did we.

A question asked in Zen Buddhism is, "What is the most valuable part of a bowl?" The answer is its emptiness. Without its functional emptiness it would lose its identity as bowl.

♦ Victoria Moran, *Shelter for the Spirit*

35

Pottery

◆ ◆ ◆

POTTERY HAS LONG BEEN A LOVE OF MINE. DESIRING to become a potter myself, years ago I enrolled in a class. Twice I fell off the wheel. I attributed this to my enthusiasm and focused attention on the clay that was spinning in front of me. The instructor said no one had ever fallen off the wheel in his class. His look and words made me feel like a failure. In and of itself, this was probably not a sign that becoming a potter was unlikely, but I was discouraged. Hearing of my disappointment, a friend suggested a most helpful reframe. Potters need someone to buy their pots. Me! That could be me! That was me!

I relish every form of pottery and find it difficult to rein in my need for yet another bowl, mug, tray, unusual vessel. Sometimes I wonder if this is considered an addiction like women who buy shoes or men who buy tools. The next is always needed, desired, the perfect elixir to the wanting heart. Being on the art show circuit, imagine the amazing and talented potters I have come to know. Each piece I purchase is like a friendship.

Simplicity had pottery everywhere. One acquisition was a playful clay house that both inspired and motivated me to write about Simplicity, as well as to create distinctive and whimsical buildings in my paintings. This piece sat on a shelf in my office. Residing on another bookshelf was an elongated bowl of sorts, sculpted as a goose. Rocks from our travels filled this unusual vessel.

Most of our pottery had a function. I find the words of Lao Tzu written in the Tao Te Ching both philosophical and practical. "We shape clay into a pot, but it is the emptiness inside that holds whatever we want." When opening Simplicity's kitchen cupboards, I saw clay friends waiting for soup, salads, coffee, and more. Their emptiness accommodated our many needs.

With an abundance of serving bowls, several were rerouted into a different use. Both bathrooms had deep bowls that held items for the bath. Make-up items were gathered in a cracked bowl that could no longer hold liquid or be safe in its use with food, but was perfect in this new supporting role. My bangle bracelets rested in a bowl with a pattern of the potter's thumbprints on the outside. Some bowls held a burning candle or my pens and markers. Others held onions, garlic, squash, and sweet potatoes in the kitchen. Their service to our home was invaluable, adding interest and beauty.

One anniversary, Don and I celebrated by purchasing a set of dinnerware from a potter whose square plates were most distinctive. When the order was ready, she offered to meet us halfway. I responded with gratitude for her willingness to accommodate this transfer and asked if it would be possible to come to her studio. I further explained that these were not just dishes we had ordered, but they were part of an expression of creativity that would enhance our table, our hospitality, our lives. To see where and how they were made was important in honoring their intention in our home. When we arrived at the studio, the potter took us through her process of birthing these uniquely shaped plates, each with a slightly dissimilar glaze dripping from her artist's touch.

One potter wisely said to her students, "Try to put thought, time and care into making these useful objects with the hopes that the users will somehow connect with them beyond their intended purpose." Our clay bowls, trays, mugs, and whimsical house added quality to living in Simplicity. They enhanced our days with a helpful function and added beauty. From the earth, shaped in the hands of the potter, then brought into our home, each piece brought a holiness to grace our lives. Each empty bowl offered the capacity to hold the unknown.

Cupboard: A piece of furniture with a door and usually shelves used for storage.

◆ Concise Oxford
English Dictionary

36

The Tall Blonde

◆ ◆ ◆

A TALL CUPBOARD STOOD QUIETLY IN THE CORNER of Simplicity's kitchen. The light from the long windows suited her, enriched her ash blonde coloring. Placed at an angle to the corner of the room, she stood out, announcing herself. But then, this was her cunning personality.

Don was the first to greet her in the morning, often before daylight entered the room. The coffee maker cuddled onto one of her shelves. This was where she and Don met—in the mornings over coffee while I was still asleep.

When we purchased the tall blonde, I had no idea she would favor Don over me. While that happens with his and her chairs—different body types needing different comforts—this was totally unexpected from a cabinet. They bonded from the beginning.

She came into our life when we moved into apartment 2B as a most efficient solution for our computer needs. I now know that I was naive to think of her as only a computer cabinet. Did Don see more in her at their first encounter or was it a gradual affair? Either way, it took place right under my nose and totally without suspicion.

When we moved into Simplicity, the tall blonde

came with us. Don reworked her job description and soon she was employed as an entertainment center. With her long lanky doors, she could easily hide things. At the time, I saw this as one of her virtues. In retrospect, I see the progression of her patient plotting and deliberate ploy into Don's life. Did he not see her coy manipulation?

As the years passed, the tall blonde was no longer needed as an entertainment center. Don was quick to suggest her valuable contribution to the kitchen. His plan included simple cosmetic surgery with hooks installed to hang pots and pans. Pullout shelves could house trays and griddles. Behind those lanky doors, the coffee maker and blender had special places to live. Wine bottles and glasses were an easy reach within her interior world. Assisting our day-to-day kitchen routines was worthy work. The loud banging and cumbersome sorting to find a pan or a blender were gone, problem solved. Once again, the tall blonde's diverse resume and dependable service were impressive. Surely, I could see that, Don insisted.

The two of them must have worked together, developing this well-conceived plan, her accommodating role in our home, in our kitchen, in my space. She knew we depended on her. Had that been her plan all along? To be indispensable? Don defended her.

For years I lived with this odd relationship between husband and cabinet. We all functioned well together. Along the way she and I developed a mutual respect for each other. Don and I never spoke of her by name. Did she have one? I wondered. While Don may have greeted her first thing in the morning, I reminded myself that I was the one he kissed good night.

When we moved from Simplicity, I told Don there

was no need to move the Tall Blonde to our new home. It was time to let her go. Once again, he insisted that she might be useful. I was certain she smirked when she heard this. So, the Tall Blonde found her place on the moving van and moved with us. Turned out she did have a new job description awaiting her. She has become my storage assistant in the studio. Her capable shelving accommodates art supplies, and her long lean doors keep the studio looking orderly. Seems she and Don no longer have a relationship. Neither one talks about the other. Both have moved on.

Your home is not just your address but also a state of mind.

♦ Winifred Gallagher, *House Thinking*

37

A House is Found

◆ ◆ ◆

DON SUGGESTED WE SHOULD START LOOKING AT houses, take our time, begin to form our intentions around where we wished to live next. We started visiting open houses. One week we focused on older houses. None impressed us. We came home to Simplicity feeling so grateful in how well she accommodated our needs. She had everything we wanted. Why were we even looking? A good question.

There was an itch to move, change up our environment, a readiness to grow ourselves in new ways. We were preparing ourselves so when the perfect house was found, we would know it. There would be clarity about what we both wanted in our next living space. We also promised ourselves that we would not leave Simplicity unless whatever was next felt just right.

What were we looking for? Another good question that kept defining itself as we looked at houses. One-story living, good light, spacious flow, an interior entryway of some kind, tall ceilings, two bathrooms, a shower and a tub, two or three bedrooms with a large master bedroom, an attached two-car garage, room for studio space. Those qualities were essential. And this time we preferred a younger home, a newer place.

Then we saw the house. Well situated on the lot, its

basic lines were dynamic and interesting. The pitch of the roof with its dormers introduced a nuance that was most appealing. A small front porch invited. While this was a one-story ranch, nothing about it reminded us of the ranch-style homes we both had lived in during our childhood years. This was new and improved. This house had energy that was contagious. This house was not boring or ordinary, but vibrant. We eagerly stepped through the front door.

Once inside, we stood in an entry that gave us room to breathe. Not large, just enough to pause and take in what was before us. The room to our right was open, did not have a door and could be used as a den, office, library, even a studio. Straight ahead was a myopic view of the great room and the outdoors seen through the expanse of windows. We decided to begin our tour by turning right, traveling through the open room, then into the classy kitchen with beautiful black appliances and a stretch of granite counters that provided plenty of workspace as well as counter seating. The great room was expansive, cathedral ceilings adding to its feel. The long sweep of the rectangular room was not daunting, but exciting to think of possibilities for its use. With an open flow, dining and living were effortless. A fireplace on one end and likely dining on the other, the room spoke of easy gatherings of people. In our minds, we began to put furniture into place.

Off the dining room was a short hallway that led to the master bedroom. Roomy enough for our bedroom furniture, a walk-in closet for far more clothing than we had, and a master bath with two sinks and walk-in shower. "Elegant convenience" was a phrase that kept repeating itself as we walked through rooms. Was this it? Was this the manifestation of our next house?

To the left of the front entry was another short

hallway with two bedrooms and a bath between. I appreciated the idea of a guest room and bath on the opposite end of the house from our bedroom. Something about this spoke of privacy for both a guest and us. The rooms were sizeable. Pleasant light came into the front room, even on a day of drizzle and dreariness. What a happy room, I thought. What joy would fill the intentions of anything that happened there. Selfishly, I knew this prime space would not be gifted to our overnight guests. The front room would be claimed for our creative thinking, used as a den or office. It was full of dreams ready to be actualized.

The bathroom on this side of the house had both a shower and a tub. Seeing the deep tub brought relief, although, I could not imagine any bathtub replacing Simplicity's claw foot. So many new homes do not have tubs, only showers. For us, a good long soak in a tub is the healing touch for a tired body, a troubled soul, a depleted spirit. A bathtub was a necessity in our home.

The back of the house looked onto a grove of trees. There was no other house or backyard to view, only a thicket of mature trees, a suggestion of being in the woods. A good sized deck off the living room offered the opportunity to be outside in nature. The space between the house and neighbors was a respectable distance. A quiet road, trees in the backyard, walking paths and sidewalks, neighbors not too close—all made for an inviting location.

This house was winning awards in my mind. I took a brief leave from tabulating details to dream, imagine life here. What would it be like to live in this house, at this location. My breath found such peace as my heart dared to live there. I could see us hosting family and friends, clients, and salon groups. Plenty of space to move furniture and people. I imagined waking up in the morning, refreshed and energetic, a lightness, a spaciousness of floor and windows to dress my day. The house recycled positive energy, refreshing itself as well as our spirits. Flow and freedom were partnered in this house. There was even space to dance!

I saw us moving in with just what we needed and loved, nothing more. A clearing out of an old life that had suited us well, with a new life awaiting us. There was room to grow something incubating within ourselves in this space. Something that had been dormant in Simplicity. Something that we trusted was there but could not be expressed, limited by our former selves, limited by boxy American Foursquare rooms.

This was the season of discernment for us. The house was larger than we needed, but it put us in a place that made our dreams feel possible. The space opened our creative juices. Our visual picture and heart-felt knowing had a shape and form that they did not have before. Our next home was out there. We were close, but not yet. A few more tomorrows were to be lived at Simplicity.

There is an atmosphere of festival, of release, in the house.

♦ May Sarton, *Journal of a Solitude*

38

Simplifying Christmas

♦ ♦ ♦

IN THE WINTER SEASON OF SPECIAL HOLIDAYS AND traditions, everyday homes are transformed into festive attire as the change of decor adds fun and significance to our lives. This environment lasts only a short while, and then it all comes down, is put away, returning us to ordinary days.

In celebrating Christmas, Don and I have tried to find just the right balance of merriment and meaning to suit our style of decor and Simplicity's uniqueness. By simplifying what she wore, three basic accessories adorned Simplicity for the season: red berries, the Spode Christmas dishes, and a wreath.

Abundant red berries are my favorite trimming for numerous places in Simplicity. The first to find their designated location were positioned above the white kitchen cabinets. Sprouts of red berries jump out of the handmade pottery along the cabinet tops. How I loved those artificial sprigs of red that offered whimsy to a white winter, sprinkling Simplicity with dots of festivity. Other strings of berries were draped over mirrors, the entrance to the dining room, around lamps.

The Christmas dishes have been collected over time. Each year a piece of the Christmas Tree pattern was added until we had enough place settings, serving dishes, and cups with saucers. Meals, desserts and coffee served during the holiday used the Christmas Spode. Everything tasted better and felt like a party.

After a few years with a natural tree, we acquired a hand-me-down artificial tree from my father. Quickly, we discovered how much easier it was to put up and pack away; plus it was economical. When the tree began to look sad and worn out, we sat with the question of having any kind of tree. The iconic Christmas symbol was up for discussion. A tree took up sizeable space in Simplicity. Where to place the tree was complicated by the number of doors and windows, as well as the traffic pattern of our floor plan. To eliminate a Christmas tree from our holiday decor felt untraditional, as if we were traitors to the season. Then there was the question of what to do with the tree ornaments filled with memories. Where would they go without a tree?

We thought long and hard on this and finally decided that a large artificial wreath on the wall could hold many of the cherished ornaments gathered over the years. We liked the idea that a circle of greens is honored as a symbol of peace. We appreciated that the circle is universally found in all cultures and holds similar meanings of unity and wholeness. With our country struggling to find a sense of inclusivity and respect, the diversity of ornaments brought a richness to our lives, reminding us to honor differences as gifts to the whole.

The wreath was strung with small white lights that danced among our favorite ornaments. Being the one most hesitant about this bold change to eliminate a tree, I had to admit that the Christmas spirit was still present. I felt the same amount of joy in my heart when I came down the stairs in the morning to a lighted wreath of wonder. The first light to be lit in the morning and the last to be unplugged in the evening, the wreath held memories and hope. Sprinkled here and there were other indications of the holiday, but Christmas wasn't Christmas at Simplicity without red berries, the Spode dishes, and the Christmas wreath.

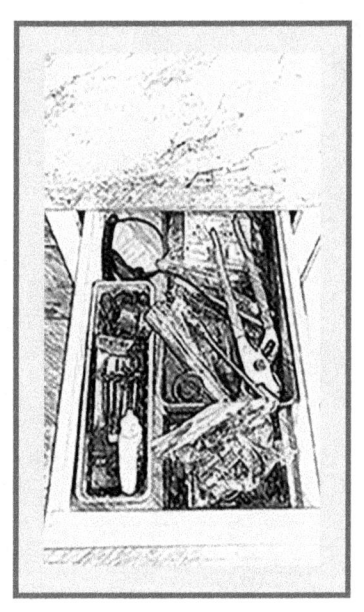

Every house needs a junk drawer.

♦ Don Mendenhall

39

More Than a Junk Drawer

◆ ◆ ◆

IT STARTED WITH AN INNOCENT CONVERSATION over morning coffee about something rather insignificant—the junk drawer. When we first moved into Simplicity, Don asked for a designated junk drawer in the kitchen. While I occasionally used this drawer, it was Don's domain. He was the sole proprietor and manager of its contents.

"My dad had a junk drawer," Don randomly shared during our morning conversation. "And my grandfather. I remember as a child how I loved to look in them. Felt like a treasure hunt, never knowing what I would find. Both were messy and chaotic. That's what made them a great junk drawer. Junk drawers are messy."

"Really?" I inquired, as I thought of my childhood experience with a junk drawer. "My dad's junk drawer wasn't messy. Seemed organized. Dad labeled everything. He had little jars and metal containers marked for paper clips, rubber bands, brads, tacks. There were boxes and plastic bins that organized all the other containers. I loved looking in the drawer that held fun pens, small screwdrivers, and measuring tapes with different advertising on them. I felt important, thinking of all the ways things could be used."

I paused, now giving further thought to this little

drawer in Simplicity's kitchen. "What is a junk drawer for?" I asked the resident expert sitting across from me.

"I think the junk drawer is about efficiency, easy access to something you need at a moment's notice," Don's thinking offered. He paused, then added, "It keeps things safe. This is the place of safe keeping for procrastinations."

"Safe keeping for procrastinations?" I giggled and he did too. Did this clever phrase just spill out of his mouth or had he been thinking about this for quite some time? "Explain that to me," I encouraged him, still in amazement we were talking about a silly junk drawer. Talk about squeezing blood out of a turnip. We were squeezing and having fun.

"Well, this is where I put things like the bolt that fell out of the dining room table. I don't want to lose it because it is important. This drawer keeps it safe."

I looked at him, all pleased with himself, and loved him even more. It also crossed my mind that the bolt had been in protective custody for a very long time. Admittedly, I wondered if the mere mention of it might move the bolt from safety in the junk drawer to its rightful place in the table.

My mind was becoming intrigued with, of all things, this psyche around a junk drawer. I sipped my coffee and shifted deeper into the comfy chair. Suddenly, I felt uncomfortable. My thoughts continued. Don's junk drawer made me anxious. Not the junk drawer itself, but Don in the junk drawer. Considerable rummaging happened when Don opened it. The desperate hunt was noisy and chaotic as the contents were stirred, churned, mixed, and blended. His rustling panic made me anxious.

More coffee sipping, more thinking. I realized there was a progression to this anxiety:

1. Would he find whatever he was looking for? *Swirling and mixing heard.*

2. If not, would he head downstairs to look on the workbench? *More stirring. More rustling.*

3. If he still couldn't find what he was looking for, would he ask me? The missing item was frequently under something else, which when found, prompted a familiar response from Don. "Really? I looked there!"

4. If the item still wasn't found, the jangle of car keys was heard as he was off to the hardware store to purchase a new whatever it was.

Each of these sequential steps involved panic, noise, and a trail of disturbed drawers, bins, containers, and counter tops. That was the source of my anxiety. The pandemonium that a junk drawer—Don's junk drawer—can cause.

"Do you think everyone has a junk drawer?" I asked, thinking it a reasonable question to keep the dialog going while also circumventing the recently identified anxiety that I was not quite ready to admit to him.

"Of course," he responded. "Every house needs one."

"Are there standard items in a junk drawer?" I pushed along this curious conversation.

"Probably," he added. He started recalling the contents of Simplicity's junk drawer. Small tools like a screwdriver, hammer, and pliers. Glue. Batteries. Halogen bulbs for the light over the sink. Stoppers of various kinds. Swiss Army knives. Not junk at all, but necessary, efficient, and accessible items for times when duty calls. This drawer was a first responder in a household crisis.

That same day I was having lunch with a friend. Prompted by the morning's conversation with Don, I asked if she had a junk drawer. Indeed, she did. We exchanged the whats and whys of each item purposefully selected for this honor to be included in such an esteemed location. Then she leaned in, as if preparing to share something personal and private.

"You know, when my husband opens the junk drawer, and I hear him rummaging around, I get anxious."

"You do?" my surprise and selfish delight showed. My secret anxiety had just been affirmed and confirmed.

She continued, "There is always a chance he won't find what he is looking for and then he will call me to help. Why I can easily find whatever it is in such a small space and he cannot is a mystery to me."

A knowing smile came across my face, wondering if we were only talking about junk drawers.

Comfort—the passive enjoyment of the home by its owners. Convenience—the proper functioning of the house.

◆ Robert Kerr, Architectural Historian, from *Home,* by Witold Rybczynski

40

Jinxed

◆ ◆ ◆

I PULLED THE CHAIN. THE FLUSHING LEVER WOULD not budge. The toilet was broken. A house with five overnight guests for two days and the toilet was not working. I climbed on top of the toilet seat, reached close to the ceiling to remove the tank cover from our European-style water closet. Not enough headroom to look inside. Reaching into the tank, I felt a broken chain. An attempt to blindly attach it to the lever failed. I jotted "broken" on a sticky note and stuck it to the toilet seat.

Returning to my place at the dining room table where our guests were playing a game, I announced, "The toilet is broken. Please use the one upstairs." Sympathetic faces looked at mine. Only Don's showed panic. "I know," my eyes said back to him. "An awful time to have this happen." Moving into handyman mode, he retrieved the ladder from the garage. Several long and involved minutes later he returned, saying a temporary fix had been found. Reminder to self—call the plumber on Monday.

No worries, no problem. Don and I knew the drill. The phrase that disasters or unfortunate events come in threes had been well achieved that year. More like multiples of threes. Not six or nine or twelve. Fifteen was the current number. We started counting after four. A year of replace and repair had found us captive. Our odd assortment of broken, repaired, and replaced items included cars, computer, snow blower, refrigerator, paper shredder, lamp, vacuum, car windshield, ceiling fans, camera, window coverings, coffee grinder, and a down comforter that suddenly lost its feathers. Most were long-lived, faithful workers up for retirement, but this felt like a labor strike.

The week following the toilet incident, I took out our blender to make a smoothie. When I pushed the button, an unfamiliar sound greeted me. There was no whirring of the fruit and yogurt. They sat still. Another try and now I was smelling smoke. Don walked into the kitchen. Our eyes connected. Really?

"Let's go buy a new one." Don's suggestion was offered with both a surrendering sigh and a readiness to improve our state of mind. With appliance and home repairs becoming quite frequent, we now engaged them as adventures.

We stood in the small appliance aisle at Target. Blenders had come a long way since we purchased ours years ago. Some just blended while others added pulsing, pureeing, grinding, even chopping. With my rule of limiting kitchen electrical devices, I had never owned a food processor. Now blenders could do it all. I read the list of promised tasks printed on the box. This was the moment I could gain two kitchen helpers for the price and storage of only one. A bonus replacement.

As soon as we walked into Simplicity with our blender purchase, a brewing thunderstorm became a full-blown hailstorm. Quarter-sized hail pelted against our gutter covers, sounding as if a machine gun were emptying its round. Now Mother Nature was adding her signature to our long list. The roof and gutter person was called the next day and came out for a quick inspection. "Your gutter covers and roof have been pummeled," he reported in a calm voice. "We'll write up a report for your insurance company." Something about the way he said pummeled reminded me it was a word I had never used. Pummeled. A word that accurately described how Don and I felt about this string of bad luck. A word I had not intended to know so intimately.

A noise in the middle of the night woke me. I nudged Don, "Did you hear that?" His groggy sleepy voice replied, "I didn't hear anything."

"Something banged, like a drawer being shut, but I hear nothing now." I settled back to sleep.

The next morning Don and I were sitting across from each other in the living room having coffee. I was recounting gratitude for the improvements we had made in the house and looked up to the recently installed ceiling fan. My face was aghast, "Don, the fan!"

The fan had pulled loose and was hanging by its wires. A jagged hole in the ceiling exposed lath and plaster. The fan itself was tipped at an angle and dangled for help. We called our electricians, reaching them on their weekend emergency number. Within minutes they arrived and assessed the situation. They relieved the fan of its air aerobics and searched inside the hole. Diagnosis—a malfunction of the fan box.

"We'll return on Monday to put in a new support. We have a drywall company we use. Happy to call them for you. After they do their work, we will return to put the fan in place." It was not their doing that was at fault. A once strong support base had pulled away. The fault lay in the exhaustion of old boards. The fan's bits and pieces covered the dining room table. There was a pause in what could be done.

We entered a waiting game. Not just for the electrician, but the plasterer, the plumber who had to return to finish work on the sump pump and toilet, a recall on our washing machine, the estimate on our roof and gutter damage. Each would bring a sense of comfort and convenience to our lives, but not at the moment.

There is a balance between what Robert Kerr called the comfort and convenience of a house. To enjoy the comfort of a home, the convenience of its living parts is a necessary function. We were inconvenienced when the refrigerator's malfunctioning thermostat required living out of ice chests. We were inconvenienced by our dismantled fan parts and a hole in the ceiling. Most days, Don and I lived our lives effortlessly in Simplicity's comfortable, convenient surroundings. We had greater appreciation for the well-functioning machines that made life in her enjoyable. I found myself saying thank you to the dishwasher, stove, furnace, water heater, microwave, television, garage doors, printers . . . Keep up the excellent work. Please do not succumb to being next on our list of disasters.

The spirit of a place inhabits it like a real dweller, and so when we are open to its presence, we feel the fullness of the space.

♦ Thomas Moore,
The Re-Enchantment of Everyday Life

41

Simplicity is For Sale

◆ ◆ ◆

SIMPLICITY WENT ON THE MARKET! WHAT? Rewind that statement. Begin again. Simplicity went on the market!

We met with our realtor friend to ask about the current housing market. Seemed like it was a wise time to sell if we could find our dream home. She sent an email about an open house of a new build in our village. That evening we rode our bikes over and looked in the windows. Nothing impressed us. We considered not going to the open house, then said to ourselves, *Everything is helpful information.*

The day of the open house was cold, gray, and rainy. Once again, seeing the front of the house said nothing exceptional to us. Then we walked in. Magic happened. The open floor plan, the volume of light coming into each room, the spirit of this modest-looking home started speaking to us, reminding us of the house we had seen earlier, but this one was just our size.

The house had details we appreciated: a separate wing for guests, cathedral ceilings in the great room, deep windowsills, a walk-in shower, a soaking tub, recessed ceiling in the master suite, kitchen cabinets with pull out drawers, a fireplace, and nine-and-a-half-foot ceilings in the unfinished basement. Excitement was building. Was this our next home?

Trying to put our eager emotions in check, we saw the sensible advantages of this house and the ease of living it offered. Family, friends, and strangers had open space to gather. Don and I could grow old here, extending our independent living. Guest accommodations tucked away from the living space felt respectful and convenient for live-in use if needed. Living on one level was practical.

Then there was the unfinished, wide open basement offering substantial studio space for both of us. Two large egress windows were in place, providing natural light. We imagined the walls as gallery space. A section of the basement could be a fun place to set up the tent for overnights with the grandchildren. Our creative souls were in a land of bliss. But before that story could unfold, dear sweet Simplicity had to find a new owner.

The first step was a photo shoot for the official listing. Her presence was confident. Her dignity strong and vital. Well loved, well maintained, and given creative license in these sixteen years, Simplicity was at her peak. She had trained for this very moment. She, too, was ready for her next life.

Our prayer for those days was:

May our decision to leave Simplicity be clear and respectful.
May our decision to purchase a new home be wise and adventuresome.
May we be at peace.

Simplicity was ready to go on the market. I casually shared with our realtor, "Wouldn't it be wonderful if the sign in the front yard could say, 'Home with a Heart for Sale.'" She surprised us! A new story had begun to unfold for both Simplicity and us.

I had walked into a room where I knew at once that much had been thought and felt, a room where books had souls, where life was lived at great intensity in the silence.

♦ May Sarton, *Plant Dreaming Deep*

42

Love Letter to Simplicity

◆ ◆ ◆

SIMPLICITY RECEIVED A LOVE LETTER IN THE MAIL. A young woman and her family visited during the open house and fell under the magical spell of this old house. Her finances did not afford the possibility to purchase, but that did not stop her from sharing her feelings.

> On our family's journey to find our perfect first home, we came across Simplicity online. Looking at pictures, we loved the simple beauty of your home. Knowing it was over our price range, I had to convince my boyfriend to "just look" at the open house. As my boyfriend, daughter, and I walked up to the porch and through your home, we fell in love with every creaky step, as Simplicity told us her love story. My best girlfriend said, "When you see the one, you will feel it." I didn't understand what she meant until we experienced it. We were overwhelmed by the perfection of Simplicity. Simple understated elegance. I understand I am breaking the rules by sending this, but I thought I'd extend our love for your home. Whoever takes on the life of Simplicity couldn't be luckier.

Simplicity was deeply loved. I received requests from friends who wished to come say a last goodbye, to offer gratitude for times shared in her rooms, to linger with us in her caring spaces. And I wondered, how does one say goodbye to a faithful and dear friend? How does one recall all the stories of living here that fill countless chapters of our lives? How do we say thank you?

The house itself welcomed us.
♦ May Sarton,
Journal of a Solitude

43

SOLD!

◆ ◆ ◆

SIMPLICITY SOLD. I NEEDED TO LET THE REALITY soak in. She would have new owners. We would be moving out. Our relationship with this dear house was to end.

Within a whirlwind of days we found our ideal home, submitted an offer, put Simplicity on the market, had an open house and showings, and she sold. Our hearts and stomachs had one wild ride. Every possible emotion was squeezed from our bodies: fear, anxiety, excitement, relief, sadness, joy, anticipation, worry, and more. The nights, when the heart and mind had time to ponder, were sleepless. The days, when the body and mind were overly active, managed the million details in those transactions. Exhaustion was the result. Nothing felt simple, light, playful. Not yet.

In the midst of overwhelm was also deep gratitude. Simplicity's new owners sounded like they were hand-picked. Their realtor shared with ours:

> *My couple fell in love with the character of the home, as well as its story. It reminded them of the houses they grew up in, and they love what your Seller has done with it. They hope to*

build on it for their time there, as their family grows!"

Sitting in Simplicity, I heard her confidence that all was just as it should be. It was time for us to leave. Time for others to move in. Once again, Simplicity would offer herself to be molded and shaped by the lives of her new owners. This was part of her DNA, her personality. This was her gifted nature.

Don and I were thankful for the professionals who guided us, gave us courage to carry on, and answered the questions that muddled our brains. An entourage of well-informed specialists calmed our nerves, heard our stories, and earned our trust. Each day another checkmark or two or three was made beside a list of looming tasks. Each day the overwhelm found a bit of release and the sense of adventure wiggled through a crack.

The immediate days ahead found us asking questions about what should go, what should stay. Boxes of every shape and size were our constant companions. Order turned into chaos. We lived in the temporary state of in-between.

We asked our realtor how long we had been searching for our next home. She replied, "My notes go as far back as five years." But I knew the undocumented notes went back much further. The journey to find home, our next home, had been lengthy. We had been intentional in our search, our demands of a house, and the kind of lifestyle we desired to live. Our refrain became: *we will know it when we see it*.

In talking with our realtor, I made reference to "our house." When asked for clarification as to which house I was referring, Simplicity or the one we were buying, I realized I was speaking of the new house. Somewhere between the past and the future, the house that sat on the bend of a road had become home, the house in which we chose to live our lives forward. I remembered our prayer: May our decision to leave Simplicity be clear and respectful. May our decision to purchase a new home be wise and adventuresome. May we be at peace.

The space for what you want is already filled with what you settle for instead.

♦ Stephen C. Paul,
*Illuminations—Visions for Change,
Growth, and Self-Acceptance*

44

Downsizing?

◆ ◆ ◆

AN ASSUMPTION AS TO WHY WE WERE SELLING Simplicity was that we were downsizing. Ever so quickly that word landed in the conversation and sat uncomfortably. Somehow downsizing made our move understandable. This has become a norm, even an expectation, that at a certain age one changes the size of dwelling space and number of possessions. While downsizing may make sense to people about our reason for moving, it was not accurate.

Downsizing frequently means a letting go, a simplifying, a lessening of the household responsibilities, a smaller space. I must admit that this part was true for us. We were letting go of furniture and household items. Craigslist was a helpful partner. With each sale, we sent off a part of our former lives where it was given new life with different owners. Family heirlooms that had been well loved in Simplicity, but did not fit our perceived life at our new home, found family members who would delight in their opportunity to enjoy them. There was something very satisfying about this kind of letting go.

Sorting through stuff means sorting out life. We were letting go of many previous lives to make space for the life that was before us. Unless an item had a useful purpose or would bring energy to our new life, it would not travel with us. As an item left our possession, a space opened to dream in expanded ways.

Don's and my morning conversations about what we would not take with us included emotional habits. I would try to leave my extensive box of worries and competitive comparisons behind. Don was committed to not rushing through life, choosing to live in the moment. Naming these was helpful and clarifying. While an old habit is hard to break, at least we would give each of these our mindful attention and best effort.

Simplicity had given us her best effort, reached her limit to handle our needs and requests. I, too, had reached my limit. The difficulty of fitting life in those boxy rooms and adding more light had exhausted me. To ask Simplicity for more light and flexibility meant knocking out walls and changing her very character. I remembered my promise to never change her basic bone structure. Both of us had reached the capacity of our ability to honor the other.

The word downsizing can also be attached to a lifestyle that is quieter and less involved. For some, leaving a place they love is painful, as if a part of life had been taken away, even diminished by this act of downsizing. Perhaps this was where I felt the rub. Everything about the move was about growing ourselves and expanding our possibilities. When we walked into our new home, we instantly felt its spaces ready to assist, support, and encourage our next stage of life. The new home opened a whole new world for our creative energies, marriage, and opportunity to explore other parts of who we were.

As Don said, "This move is almost like changing cultures." Going from an American Foursquare to a twenty-first-century ranch was a dramatic change of living environment. In nearly every way, the new house was the exact opposite of Simplicity.

What awaited us? A life where our daily patterns would be influenced by new spaces. Where we would have coffee, how we would answer the door, hang up our coats, do laundry, what we would see out the window, how we would place our furniture—everything would be different from Simplicity.

"It is likely that even our conversations will change," Don added. I understood exactly what he meant. No longer would we talk about how to make changes in Simplicity to fulfill our needs or where we would live next or would we ever find a place that fit us. The house on the bend of the road would fill us with new energy, new thoughts, new understandings, new conversations.

Within days of moving into our new home, we celebrated our twentieth anniversary. Another reset of life. A threshold moment that held both the gift of a known history together and an unknown future before us. The unknowns were wrapped in a package of wonderful wild escapades to be lived and discovered. Nothing about this felt like downsizing.

Our homes and our relationships to them become especially important and revealing when our lives are in a state of transition.

◆ Winifred Gallagher, *House Thinking*

45

Waiting Anxiously

◆ ◆ ◆

Two companions—Waiting and Anxiety—joined us during our days of house selling and house buying. Their close friend—Overwhelm—was nearby. Both Don and I are people who take responsibility, make things happen. Yet much of the situation was out of our control. Documents went to underwriters or to third parties or to someone in the internet family. Then we waited for their approval or signature or returned with additional information. Everything had a process, a known protocol. There was an intense timeliness to this buy and sell process. I felt out of breath without doing anything physical.

My mind spun and looped around for yet another quote, question, task. It felt endless. With each transaction in the sale of Simplicity or the purchase of the new home, we were grateful for a gifted real estate agent. Without her we would have been sitting on a whole bunch of questions and moving nowhere.

Still, we waited. We waited . . . anxiously.

Timeliness had never felt more important. A hailstorm in May damaged our roof. We did not rush to replace it. We had no idea we would be moving so quickly. With the sale of Simplicity, a new roof and gutters were mandatory. Instantly, an inspector, an insurance claim, and a roofing outfit that had an opening before the end of October were crucial to the sale of the house. It seemed all would happen in the shortened time frame, but not without anxious waiting. Once the insurance check arrived, our nerves calmed. Restlessness then transferred its energy to the many more unknowns still deserving of diligent worrying.

Deep breath.

Due to the quick pace of Simplicity's sale and a backlog of available appraisers, the appraisal was completed after our sale price was agreed upon by the buyer. Friends of Waiting and Anxiety—Restlessness and Worry—wondered if our selling price had been in the ballpark. The appraisal arrived. Once again, all was well, but not without our minds dashing back and forth with projected problems and possible delays.

Another deep breath.

Early in the process we worried whether this quirky older home would even sell. Being an unusual house, finding the right buyer could have been a challenge. Once again, timeliness was important. We required a buyer who was not waiting to sell a house, had been pre-approved by the bank, and was ready to move in October. That very scenario happened. The process continued to find the magic.

After we said YES to our new home, the ball started rolling, taking us with it. Everything about the move felt right, timely, and perfect. Our excitement bordered on giddiness. Our energy exploded with creative thoughts. Still, the days of waiting anxiously were where we lived. We were in this land of in-between, a land where we were not in charge, but had to trust and rely on the expertise of people we had just met, whose voices we had come to know by phone. They were the ones who steadied our nerves, handled our barrage of questions, and reminded us that this was nothing out of the ordinary. Their ordinary was our extraordinary.

Deep breath.

More boxes to pack. We were running low. A quick call was made to my new friend in the produce department at Pick 'n Save. He saved the sturdy fruit boxes for me. I paused to think of all the new people we had met since the moving process began. Their smiles and helpfulness tempered our anxiety, calmed our fears. The phone rang. The roofer said the crew would be here on Monday. Another worry found relief. Such good people working on our behalf.

Deep breath.

Deep gratitude.

We need our places and times of sanctuary. We bring our serenity and happiness into whatever situation we find ourselves.

> ♦ Anne Wilson Schaef,
> *Living in Process—Basic Truths
> for Living the Path of the Soul*

46

Living In-Between

♦ ♦ ♦

WE WERE LIVING IN THE LAND OF IN-BETWEEN. Not yet in our new home. Not fully in Simplicity. Boxes surrounded us. Lists were endless. Tasks seemed overwhelming. We could not help but imagine our lives in the new house. There was both excitement and curiosity in the many unknowns before us.

In dismantling Simplicity, we were also dismantling our current life, finding ourselves letting go with each box we packed. Experiencing Simplicity's walls without artwork, floors without rugs, shelves without dishes, we wondered how best to live in this land of in-between. Don and I cozied into the two ends of our sofa with mugs of hot coffee. The two upholstered chairs where we used to sit for our morning chats were no longer in the room. They and the rug that tied everything together were gone, sold on Craigslist. There was an absence of the familiar, replaced by stacked cardboard boxes. Living this way was unsettling.

As we sipped coffee, a temporary solution was found. Don recommended we create one room, the living room, that would keep us grounded, at peace, and would have a sense of order. Artwork remained on the walls, just the right number of lamps and end tables found a common purpose, the room was kept tidy. The neighboring dining room turned into a staging area. A standing screen shielded our view of the growing stacks of boxes filling this space.

The smaller size of the dining table hugged a wall in the living room. A small lamp spilled light onto the table and the painting above. This was a favorite positioning of the dining room table for me as I often thought of myself sitting in the dining car of a train or at a grand hotel. Rather than feeling misplaced, I felt elegant. With the absence of our kitchen table, sold on Craigslist, all meals happened at the table in the living room. This practical setup exuded a coziness for the entire room.

An ivy plant and our black Buddha statue were the only two accessories in this room. The rest had been packed away. The plant grounded me and gave me peace. The Buddha, with his calm demeanor and toes sticking out from under his frock, brought humor and enchantment. Both offered good reminders for living in this land of in-between.

A house that does not have one worn, comfy chair in it is soulless.

♦ May Sarton, *Journal of Solitude*

47

From Katharine to Phoebe

◆ ◆ ◆

ONE OF MY CONSTANTS IN LIFE WAS NESTLING into the comfy Katharine Hepburn chair. When I was first divorced and moved into a house that held me well, I purchased her. An admirer of Katharine Hepburn as a strong and independent woman, the house and chair were symbols of these qualities. For years, Ms. Hepburn and I lived well together.

I called Ms. Hepburn the do-nothing chair. Most La-Z-Boys recline or swivel or have buttons that do things. The Katharine Hepburn chair did nothing. She simply sat beautifully. One's legs could be tucked underneath, thrown over the arms, or crossed in a yoga pose. She offered space to get comfortable with a book, a journal, or a conversation with a friend. As Don and I prepared for the move and made decisions on what went and what did not, we noticed her worn body. She needed a new cushion and fabric.

Our plan was to have Ms. Hepburn reupholstered. Asking around, we learned that to do this was twice the cost of a new chair. Being practical people on this issue, we began a search for her replacement. We visited the La-Z-Boy store and asked for a do-nothing chair. The description required an explanation for our puzzled salesperson. After an amused smile and agreement that this was a pretty good definition of such a chair, she acknowledged that there were only a few from which to choose. This was how we met Phoebe, a name given by La-Z-Boy.

To look at Phoebe was to feel your body say *ahhhhh*. Sitting in her was like falling into the most comfortable bed. Plenty of room to tuck legs underneath, to rest, to read, to ponder life. Immediately, Don and I gave her the most comfortable chair award. She was the one! The right size, the right shape, with plenty of fabric choices to suit our new house decor. Who knew that grass would be in our color vocabulary, sharing a room with kiwi and crayola? The new house would have a different vibe than Simplicity, but one thing was for sure, a comfy chair would await one and all, whether short or tall, young or old. Just like her predecessor, Phoebe would become a well-loved and soulful presence in our home.

Remember me.
Love, Simplicity

◆ Susan Eaton Mendenhall

48

One Happy House Left

◆ ◆ ◆

A COINCIDENCE? A HAPPENSTANCE? A WONDER, for sure. How did a painting of a house that looked like Simplicity end up being the last, the only one left? Of the twenty-five I painted, how did this become the only one not sold, not selected, not chosen? A mystery to me.

I called this portfolio of artwork *Happy Houses*—small, two-and-a-half-inch square renditions of quirky looking townhouses, apartments, brownstones, cottages, bungalows, cabins, two-story and ranch-style homes. The colors and unusual lines enhanced their whimsy. Who paints a roof yellow, a chimney purple, a front door lime green? Who creates a house with a wonky roof, a street that looks like a zipper, windows shaped as odd triangles? Jazz the artist does. Only the painted ladies of San Francisco come close to this kind of playfulness. These multi-style places to call home were showcased in six-inch burnished copper frames. Each painting was positioned off center, which added to their appeal.

They were an immediate hit at art shows. Unique, stunning, not found in stores, the frames quickly sold the Happy Houses they displayed. Comments from the delighted buyers were first about the frames, then about the paintings. I tried not to be offended. This played out in hushed conversations between women friends as they stood in my booth, totally within earshot of me, the artist.

"What a gorgeous frame. You know what you could do, Jane? Buy it and put your own picture in it."

That was how I knew what became of some of the Happy Houses once they were purchased. Some of the paintings and their stunning frames were truly happy being purchased as housewarming gifts, just as I intended. Others were soon to feel a sense of responsibility by holding a family photo. All were sold, gone off to new homes, except for one. When I noticed it alone on the shelf, I did a double take. It looked like Simplicity. Two-story, yellow house with a green roof. A simple description I had given countless times to identify the real Simplicity.

I have no memory of painting this sweet whimsical version of Simplicity. Was there a reason it was left behind, not purchased, lingered longer than the others? Perhaps this particular house was not as quirky as the others, assuming that quirkiness was the reason they sold to begin with, which could be a flawed rationale. Perhaps an orange background was not a desirable color. Perhaps those who came to my art shows knew through cosmic communication that I was writing about a house named Simplicity, and this is what she looked like, and they decided to leave this one for me, for inspiration, to be my muse. Perhaps this painting always landed in the back row, unnoticed, overlooked, a wallflower among the other Happy Houses. Perhaps it just happened, in delightful play, while the house gods were moving furniture; the spirit of Simplicity sent a copper-framed telegram to the one writing her story saying, *Remember me.*

We shape our buildings and then our buildings shape us.

♦ Winston Churchill

49

Saying Good-Bye

◆ ◆ ◆

DUST BUNNIES DANCED ACROSS THE EMPTY wooden floors, evading my woolen dust mop. It felt like a game of hide-and-seek, except there was no place to hide. All the furniture had been packed on the moving truck. The final task was cleaning the floors, making sure nothing was left behind.

My dust mop paused as I remembered Don's words shared over coffee that morning. "I think of Simplicity as a gift. A gift we were given. A gift we are giving to another. I look around and see all the ways we made this house a home."

When we met Simplicity, we were at the beginning of our marriage, new careers, and artistic endeavors. We had hopes to grow well together in a place we could call home. Simplicity's emptiness was a white canvas on which to paint our lives and dreams. She provided plenty of room for possibilities and patience for our unknowns to be discovered. Getting ready to leave, her vacated rooms were full of stories and experiences: the day we met house number five; the months our son and family lived with us; the overnight stays by friends and family; finding studio spaces to create; the smell and sound of coffee brewing for our morning chats; the porches where we took deep breaths with our thoughts;

watching the squirrels at play in the trees; and hearing the birds call to each other.

No room, no space was truly empty.

In every other home, I have walked through the vacant rooms before moving, giving thanks to the spaces for their service to our lives. There was no need here. Simplicity lived inside me from day one. In so many ways we grew up together, like siblings. She shaped our marriage, was my partner in designing two businesses, was a mentor in minimalism and a safe place for my struggles. She offered flexible space for artistic pursuits and was always a teacher who asked, *What do you need of me? Let's make it happen.*

I did not retrace my steps on that final day. While the rooms were empty, my heart was bursting with memories and immense gratitude.

I felt Simplicity nudge me toward the door.

I need some quiet time to get ready for the new owners, I heard her say. *You have received all I can give and now a new life awaits us. There is no sorrow in this parting, no longing or regrets. Both of us have clarity about who we are and what we are called to do. Let's go make that happen.*

With one last sweep of the dust mop and a deep sigh, I closed the door. She would sleep alone that night. Her new owners would arrive in the morning. She would begin a new chapter of life, just as we would.

Goodbye, dear Simplicity. There is no way to measure our gratitude

Your home is an evolving creative being. It can be introverted or it can be outgoing. It has cycles just as you and all of nature has cycles.

♦ Denise Linn, *Sacred Space*

50

Each House Holds a Story

◆ ◆ ◆

Each of the houses I have lived in has supported me in significant ways. The relationship with each one transformed it into a home, as well as transformed me. This reciprocal transformation, I imagine, happens to each one of us when our hearts and souls open to the places where we live. One house leads to the next, like a residential street of driveways and learnings, as we build our understanding of house and resident.

My childhood house, a gray asbestos-shingled ranch with white trim, was located across from the elementary school I attended. In my thirties, my father and I had the opportunity to walk through this home when it was up for sale. He was shocked that so many of the built-ins he designed for our family's needs were still in place: the bookcase divider in the living room, the cupboard over the tub, a fold down desk in the den. The rooms and the backyard seemed small to me. The life I remember living there was so large, how could it have fit into these spaces? Each day of my childhood I pretended I was someone whose life I yearned to live, even keeping a diary listing their names. I decorated my room to suit the person I pretended to be: Lucy of *I Love Lucy*; detective Nancy Drew, a character I found in a book, an older girl I worshiped; many days I was Zorro, a cowgirl, a circus performer. This was the house where I jumped out of my bedroom window onto my awaiting horse—a broom from the garage. My childhood house was about growing up, learning who I was as a member of a family, being a girl, and exploring my imagination.

When I was in high school, my family built a house on a bluff overlooking a river. This serene location provided a calming place for the tumultuous years of questioning myself, entering the dating scene, and taking off for college. Here I received many accolades that fed my confidence and grew my leadership skills. I was elected captain of the cheerleaders as well as homecoming queen, performed in theater productions, asked to model for a clothing store, mentored a troubled young girl, and won the state championship in competitive swimming. These were also the years of my mother's battle with cancer and eventual death. This house held my emerging independence, a readiness to leave home, a confidence to explore more of myself. The bluff house supported the responsibility and importance of my own journey, which included letting go and seizing opportunities.

My first post-college employment was out of state. After a year, with career interests changing, I decided to return home to save money while enrolled in design classes at the local university. My homecoming was intended to be temporary; however, I was offered a job as an interior designer and stayed. I rented an apartment on the upper floor of an old house, reminding me of Mary Tyler Moore's TV apartment. Within months I met my first husband. We married and began life together in that same apartment. That was where I learned about living with a partner. No longer did I make single decisions around what belonged in our home. He loved antiques. I didn't, but his pieces were interesting and suited both of us. This little apartment provided opportunities for new conversations and compromises about sharing space and ideas. The apartment offered hands-on experience in how to create home with another.

Before long the apartment did not provide enough room for our expanding lives. We wanted more space to include a dog, a yard, and eventually, children. A two story, built in the early 1950s, became our first house, teaching us what it meant to be a homeowner. The walls required painting, the kitchen and bathroom needed to be updated, and the out-of-control yard demanded a disciplined plan with timely execution. The hours after work and on weekends belonged to the house. The 1950s house invited my repair and caretaking skills to be exercised, improved, and frequently questioned.

A gray, two-story stucco bungalow was home to the raising of our two children. Located in a college neighborhood, there were other parents with similar values. The children went to the same school, were about the same age, and friendship making was natural among the families. Winters included sledding on the hill behind the funeral home down the street, followed by gathering for hot chocolate at one of our homes. Celebrations and fun times brought us together, as did caring and helping each other in the tough times. There was a sense of completion to the child-raising years in this house, of a job well done. The gray stucco house was about motherhood and shared parenting. When we divorced, the house was sold.

What is the perfect house for a newly divorced woman? Consumed by the consequences of leaving my marriage, challenged and impassioned by my professional work, awakened and confused by becoming a single woman in her mid-forties, I longed for a home that provided grace and healing. This was found in a 1930s stucco cottage where the rooms hugged each other and me. Natural light entered in just the right places, the galley kitchen made food preparations intimate, and the large backyard with a fishpond and raised bed gardens opened me into the outdoor world. I called it the Katharine Hepburn House. Here the strong character of a favorite actress was to inspire mine. This house gave me a safe space to reflect and find new beginnings. The Katharine Hepburn House held my journey into the second half of life.

Falling in love and marrying Don eventually brought me to Simplicity. More than the other houses I have lived in, Simplicity became a close friend. We trusted each other, were comfortable together. She shared herself with a confident wisdom that supported our yearning to find and create home. Letting go of her was as tender as finding her. Simplicity nurtured a sense of home for our individual selves, marriage, and artistic endeavors.

It is my hope that as you have met Simplicity, you have been reminded of the houses you have lived in as well as the lessons of life each one helped shape and support in you. The houses I have lived in have graciously provided a space for me to learn and grow myself awake. Each has been a marriage of sorts, a give and take, for better or worse. Each house became a home. For them all, I am grateful.

Homes, Gamache knew, were a self-portrait. A person's choice of color, furnishing, pictures. Every touch revealed the individual.... He felt a thrill every time he entered a home during an investigation.

♦ Louise Penny, *Still Life*

Epilogue

◆ ◆ ◆

For a few years I volunteered with Habitat for Humanity by offering a workshop called Making a House a Home. It was optional, set aside from the required classes on how to budget, what to know about the furnace and water heater, and general house maintenance. Sometimes a family taking my workshop had already moved into their home, but most were still spending evenings and weekends putting in the required labor getting their house ready. They came to my workshop tired, yet committed. The day of owning a house was a dream come true.

The style of my workshop was conversational. I began by asking for a definition of home. As my participants reflected, I found they dug down into their vision for how this house would change their lives. The weariness of the day was slowly replaced with anticipation as they transported themselves into a new neighborhood and their very own house on the block. Thoughtfully, they began defining home:

- home is about being able to be who you really are

- a home provides privacy

- home means having a sense of freedom

- home is a place to call your own

- home is where family gatherings happen

- a home creates a cozy feeling

- a home brings peace and comfort into our lives

- a home is a haven, a place where you feel safe

Thinking of the ordinary and familiar aspects of daily life, I invited them on a mental walk-through of their new home.

- How will you enter your home on a regular basis? What needs to be there to support your comings and goings?

- What multiple activities will be happening in the living room, the dining room, the kitchen? How will the space be organized to accommodate this?

- What special furniture, art, or memorabilia will enhance your spaces? What does it say about who you are? Where will it be placed?

- How will you live in the outdoor spaces? What is needed to make that happen?

- What colors are you planning to paint the walls and have around you? Why those colors?

- What personality do you wish each room to express and how will this be accomplished?

- What room do you think will be your favorite and why?

As they shared, I watched the group gain energy and wisdom from each other. With each question they went deeper into their new home and the details of the life they would live there. In some ways the process was asking: *What is it that you need from this house to be the best and happiest you? How can your home support your life? How do you want home to feel when you walk into each room?*

In naming what would be packed from their current space for the new home, an equally important decision was what would not be moving. Stories were shared of a readiness to let go and start fresh.

"I have seen the last of that sofa! I never liked it."

"Our whole family is de-cluttering. Even the children are making decisions about what toys will go and what ones will not."

"This is a new beginning. I'm leaving most everything behind."

Within the process was a natural sorting of memories related to household pieces as well as identifying daily habits. Each homeowner was awake to the hopes and dreams they were placing in this new living space.

Wanting to keep this intention alive and active, I offered several homework suggestions to take into their home.

- Walk through your house. Name what speaks of your values and beliefs.

- List objects that have special meaning for you.

- Give thought to how you wish each room to be "at its best" for your daily living.

- Identify where clutter happens. Decide how to organize or let go of items.

- Give thanks for your home, treating it with respect and appreciation.

In the closing minutes of class, I asked the homeowners to think of their house as if it were a person, even consider whether they, too, might gift their house a name.

"What do you want to say to your home? What do you hear it saying to you?" I asked.

There was silence in the room. They took their time, measured their thoughts, and when they spoke, it was with gentle voices.

> Homeowner: "I am so grateful for you."
> Home: "Thank you for your loving work in creating me."
>
> Homeowner: "I am nervous about maintaining you, but I will do my best."
> Home: "We will learn together."
>
> Homeowner: "We have so many hopes and dreams for our family. You are a very important part of our story."
> Home: "I wish to support your dreams."

Our homes help us to know ourselves. Simplicity was a great teacher and caring mentor. Because of the questions we asked her—and our new home, Rumley—our homes have been supportive and accommodating of our needs and desires.

Discussion Questions for Book Groups or Personal Reflection

◆ ◆ ◆

1. What was your first impression of the book?
2. Is there a specific story that spoke to you? Why?
3. Each story begins with a black-and-white image and a quotation. Was a particular image or quotation helpful to your understanding of the story that followed?
4. The author shared that as she came to understand her home, she came to understand herself. Where do you see this happening?
5. How would you describe the relationship between the author and Simplicity?
6. Simplicity is given a personality and a voice. How does this help you know her?
7. Throughout the book, the author speaks of the changes made in the house to accommodate their lives and dreams. Where has this been evident in your life with your home?
8. For more ideas for discussion, read "Conversation Starters," starting on the next page.

I had first to dream the house alive inside myself.

> ♦ May Sarton,
> *Plant Dreaming Deep,*

Conversation Starters

◆ ◆ ◆

THERE IS A GOOD CHANCE THAT READING THIS book will get you thinking about your own house and home. Perhaps you'll start to feel that it is time to make a few changes to improve your "home" situation—maybe by rearranging furniture, rethinking how space is used, inviting new activities and traditions to celebrate your partnership with your house. Here are some questions you may wish to ask yourself or other people living in your house to help you to focus on where enhancements might be needed.

1. What is your definition of home?
2. Have you ever lived in a place that was truly you? Describe.
3. What spaces are working well in your current home? What spaces are frustrating? Why?
4. Where is space wasted?
5. What spaces in your home do you wish to be public? private? formal? informal?
6. Is flexibility important in your home? Where?
7. Where do you regularly enter your home? Is this entrance pleasurable? If not, what would make it more so?

8. What furniture is especially important to you and why?
9. If you have family heirlooms, do they feel like an honor or a burden?
10. What furniture, decor, or art do you no longer wish to include in your living spaces?
11. What items exemplify something of your beliefs and values?
12. What would make your home more reflective of you?
13. What in your home interests you and those who visit?
14. What in your home relaxes you and others?
15. What activities does your home need to support?
16. Where in your home do you most like to be?
17. Where in your home is natural lighting most important? Where could lamps be used more effectively?
18. What outdoor rooms enhance your life?
19. What does your home say/communicate from the outside? Inside?
20. What do you feel when you see your home from the street?
21. Describe the personality of your home.
22. Does your home have a name? Would naming it make it feel more personal?
23. If you were talking to your home as a person, what would you say to it? What would your home say back to you?

Resources

♦ ♦ ♦

I AM GRATEFUL FOR THE FOLLOWING AUTHORS WHO shaped my understanding of home and instilled in me the importance of space on our behaviors and quality of living. Each one influenced the writing of *A House Named Simplicity*.

Alexander, Christopher, Sara Ishikawa, and Murray Silverstein. *A Pattern Language: Towns, Buildings, Construction*. Berkeley, California: Center for Environmental Structure, 1968.

Alexander, Jane. *Spirit of the Home: How to Make Your Home a Sanctuary*. London: Thorsons, 1998.

Bachelard, Gaston. *The Poetics of Space*. Penguin Classics, 2014.

Bass, Diana Butler. *Grounded: Finding God in the World—A Spiritual Revolution*. New York: HarperOne, 2015.

Brand, Stewart. *How Buildings Learn* [DVD]. London: BBC, 1997.

Breathnach, Sarah Ban. *Moving On: Creating Your House of Belonging with Simple Abundance.* Des Moines, Iowa: Meredith Books, 2006.

Breathnach, Sarah Ban. *Simple Abundance: A Daybook of Comfort and Joy.* New York: Warner Books, Inc., 1995.

Busch , Akiko. *Geography of Home: Writings on Where We Live.* New York: Princeton, 2004.

Cameron, Julia. *The Artist's Way.* London: Souvenir Press, 2020.

Colwin, Laurie. *More Home Cooking: A Writer Returns to the Kitchen.* New York: Harper Perennial, 2014.

Day, Christopher. *Places of the Soul: Architecture and Environmental Design as Healing Art.* London: Taylor and Francis, 2017.

Day, Christopher. *Spirit and Place.* Architectural Press, 2002.

Gallagher, Winifred. *House Thinking: A Room-by-Room Look at How We Live.* New York: Harper Perennial, 2007.

Israel, Toby. *Some Place Like Home: Using Design Psychology to Create Ideal Places.* Chichester, West Sussex, England: Wiley-Academy, 2003.

Kingston, Karen. *Clear Your Clutter with Feng Shui.* London: Piatkus, 2017.

Lawlor, Anthony. *A Home for the Soul: A Guide for Dwelling with Spirit and Imagination*. New York: C. Potter, 1997.

Linn, Denise. *Sacred Space: Clearing and Enhancing the Energy of Your Home*. London: Rider, 2005.

Moore, Thomas. *The Re-Enchantment of Everyday Life*. Harper Perennial, 1997

Moran, Victoria. *Shelter for the Spirit: Create Your Own Haven in a Hectic World*. New York: HarperPerennial, 1998.

Oldenburg, Ray. *The Great Good Place: Cafés, Coffee Shops, Bookstores, Bars, Hair Salons, and Other Hangouts at the Heart of a Community*. Philadelphia: Da Capo Press, 2005.

Sarton, May. *Journal of a Solitude*. New York: W. W. Norton & Company, 1992.

Sarton, May. *Plant Dreaming Deep*. New York: W. W. Norton & Company, 1996.

Steele, Fritz. *The Sense of Place*. Boston : CBI Publishing Company, 1981.

Truitt, Anne. *Daybook: The Journal of an Artist*. London: Scribner, 2013.

About the Author

◆ ◆ ◆

With a lifelong interest in the places we live and work, Susan is curious about rooms, houses, and buildings and delights in discovering their personalities. Her many lives as interior designer, program director, dancer, and painter influence how she sees and uses spaces. As the former owner of a facility consulting business that interpreted the language of buildings, she writes about the ways our spaces, and what we put in them, shape and impact us.

An avid swimmer, fan of English murder mysteries, lover of strong hot coffee, storyteller, intrigued by the 1930s, admirer of Eleanor Roosevelt, creator of celebrations—Susan values simple living. Her mantra is "find the sacred in the everyday and the extraordinary in the ordinary." Susan lives with her photographer husband, Don, in their home named Rumley.

To connect, read her latest blog or explore JazzArt, please visit www.susaneatonmendenhall.com.

Shanti Arts

Nature ▪ Art ▪ Spirit

Please visit us online to browse our entire book catalog, including poetry collections and fiction, books on travel, nature, healing, art, photography, and more.

Also take a look at our highly regarded art and literary journal, *Still Point Arts Quarterly*, which may be downloaded for free.

WWW.SHANTIARTS.COM